For Albert Arsenault (1921-2004),
inventor, fisherman, and grandfather.

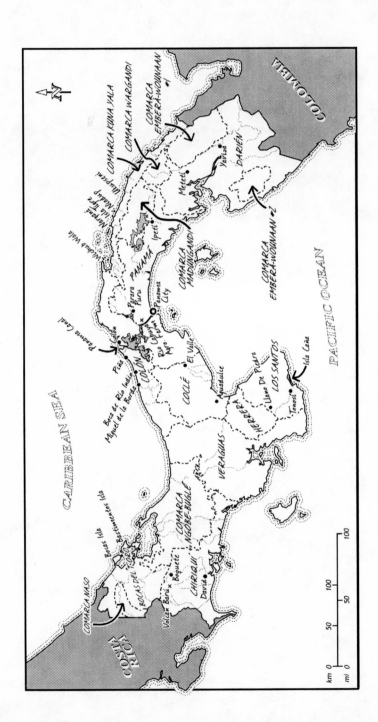

IS THERE A HOLE IN THE BOAT?

TALES OF TRAVEL IN PANAMA WITHOUT A CAR

Darrin DuFord

Acknowledgements

I would never have been able to complete this book without the help of the following people (especially those who fielded my less-than-perfect Spanish with angelic patience): Augusto Gonzalez of ANCON; Rick Morales of Ancon Expeditions; Eric Jackson, editor of *The Panama News*; the Smithsonian Tropical Research Institute's Benjamin Turner and Arcadio Castillo; Sugar Knowledge International's Phil Thompson; Daniella Zanin of the Peace Corps; Santa Rosa Refinery's Daniel Quirus; Domingo at Hotel Versailles in Chitré; Coffee Adventures' Hans van der Vooren; Panoramic Panama's Gustavo Chan; Angela Hoy from Booklocker; Eric Mercier; Curtiss Leung; and my dearest Melanie, for being unfailingly charitable about dining on whatever local fixin's were on hand during our travels.

Contents

Introduction

After the publication of my first few pieces about Panama, several of my friends began asking me when my book on the country was coming out. "I have no plans for that," I told them before my curiosity into the isthmus spawned a second visit—and then a third. And then I began asking myself the same question.

So was it the endless variety of shakes made from sensually ripe papaya, guanabana, mamey, or whatever fruits were in season? Was it the cumbia music keeping bus patrons grooving over the continental divide? Actually, the intrigue began to coalesce before my first steps in the tropical country of 3 million inhabitants—not even half the population of New York City—who are spread out over a land area that would snugly fill the largest Great Lake. While I found it a trivial task to acquire literature revealing how many gallons of water are needed to usher a ship though the locks of the country's engineering prize—an interesting metric in its own right—I encountered little written about daily lives in modern Panama. I cobbled together what I could from a backpacker's weblog here, a Peace Corps volunteer's diary there. Likewise, while its neighbor Costa Rica has been raking in tourism by the planeload, Panama still aims to expand its outside image past "a place with a canal," or, at least, past the title of a 1980s heavy metal song bearing the country's name.

And thus, little prepared me for a land where pigs going to market stand in the front of wooden canoes scantly wider than the animals' jowls as they are paddled downstream; where recycled

American school buses, painted into one-of-a-kind exhibitions, form the backbone of the country's unfathomably widespread public transport system; where I have encountered many vibrant, laughing faces of people for whom running drinkable water remains a luxury.

Slowly, however, awareness is blooming, since Panama already hosts a growing trickle of European and North American expatriates cashing in on the low cost of living. Some Zonians, or Americans who worked and lived in the former Canal Zone, have decided to remain in Panama. Tourism is beginning to expand across the country — perhaps buoyed by the recent appointment of salsa star Ruben Blades as the head of the country's ministry of tourism — yet I usually found myself as the only foreign passenger in collective boats, buses, and other improvised forms of transport. In fact, the rifle-slung police — at some of the more rural checkpoints — thought that I was either a drug dealer or a missionary entering where few foreigners care to go.

This book is a result of three separate visits between March 2004 and March 2005, with segments occurring in both the rainy and dry seasons. The chapters are in no particular order. Altogether, I spent a total of eight weeks on the isthmus, without once renting a car. Since only one in four Panamanians owns an automobile, I felt the best way to learn about the mountainous nation would be to carry on a commuting routine of a Panamanian and take the country's abundant public transportation. Even if the country was richer and car ownership proved more popular, I would still have opted for taxis and collective transit, if only for their built-in assortment of local travel companions. From a more practical standpoint, a car simply can't reach all areas of this geographically diverse nation anyway.

Since such efficiency of transport delivered me where I needed to go, the narration covers settings both urban and rural, across disparate climates and availability of basic services. You can expect regular brushes with Panamanian cuisine, the country's wildlife, and the inevitable intersection of the two.

You will also meet indigenous villages at varying levels of autonomy. But anyone who claims that the indigenous nations still existent in Panama "live just like they did when Columbus first saw them 500 years ago" is probably writing marketing copy for a travel company, especially when referring to the villages now accustomed to receiving boats full of tourists. Certainly, the time-honored architecture of thatch roof houses still abounds, but greenbacks, blue jeans, and battery-operated radios have reached all but the most isolated jungle slopes of the country. In many indigenous communities, marginalization has felled traditional sustenance. Even the Internet has arrived for some, although the villagers usually have to travel to the cities to check their email. Some call it progress; others call it cultural blanching; one thing is for sure: it's reality.

Speaking of the people, I changed the names of some folks I met in the cases where I thought one's privacy should be protected.

Lastly, this is not a guidebook; the text does not suggest what activities you should pursue while in the country, nor does it rate the softness of hotel mattresses (there are fine sources for such information elsewhere). It's about experiences and discoveries in the company of the people that are Panama.

Darrin DuFord

December 2005

IS THERE A HOLE IN THE BOAT?

TALES OF TRAVEL IN PANAMA WITHOUT A CAR

Darrin DuFord

1.
The Last Monarchy
of the Americas

"DARÍO, WE FOUND you something," echoed the morning mantra.

I looked up from a breakfast of creamed plantains as a few groundskeepers uncovered another surprise for my inspection and called out to me using the Spanish version of my name. What critter would it be this time? A bullet ant? A scorpion?

The crew waved me over to where they had accidentally exposed the current protagonist—two, actually. A snake was attempting to stretch its mouth around its own breakfast of a plum-sized frog, head first, a couple strides away from the Wekso Lodge's open-walled dining hut. The location of the lodge, up a river meandering into the forest of northwestern Panama, proved so isolated that the locale had served as the military's jungle survival training camp under Panama's dictator Omar Torrijos and strongman Manuel Noriega. The days of the camp's students washing down raw game meat with the blood of dogs at graduation have ended with Noriega's ousting in 1990, giving way to the conversion of the concrete barracks into cabanas and the area's designation as a national park, conserving all the biting wildlife you can shake a machete at.

Since the resident indigenous Naso nation has taken care of the region for centuries, the entire ecosystem has been preserved

well for this day and age.   The abundance of such arboreal
dwellers as sloths and toucans serves as a revealing sign.   At
night, sticky fingers of red-eyed tree frogs hang onto palm stalks
with bold regularity.   In fact, so much fauna resides in the forest
near the lodge that you might be inclined to suppose the
groundskeepers tied the poor creatures to the branches before an
outsider's arrival.   Such a circus of diversity bewilders not,
however, when noting that the Nasos claim a history of respecting
nature as part of their traditional sustenance lifestyles, and those I
had spoken with wanted to maintain many of their practices,
despite the recent arrival of much-enjoyed compact disc players, t-
shirts, and anything else that can fit in a dugout canoe.

While the lodge often hosts birders feverishly filling up their
checklists and biologists researching the bounty of the park, I
claimed another impetus for my five-day journey into the newly
formed autonomous region, or comarca, of the Naso nation: they
have maintained the last remaining monarchy in the Americas.
The Naso kingdom of 3,000 subjects, officially recognized by
Panama as a legal political entity, claims a distinct royal bloodline,
a palace for the king, and — like any monarchy worth its lineage —
a family feud.   In January 2005, Tito Santana, the king since 1998,
was visiting Panama City for a meeting when his uncle, Valentín
Santana, executed a coup and seized the palace.   The painful
wedge between the uncle and nephew, which has also divided the
Naso people, is the proposed construction of a dam within the
kingdom that would supply electricity to a community outside the
kingdom.

Tito was elected king seven years ago in a tradition that
allows the Naso to vote for any candidate from the Santana family
lineage.   A vigorous proponent of the dam, Tito claims that the
dam would generate income to the community and modernize the
Naso people.   Valentín, a soft-spoken elder who only speaks the

Naso language, maintains that not only will the project sire ecological disaster, but also that his nephew desires the project to pilfer most of the profits for himself. After the coup, it wasn't clear to outsiders who was currently wearing the king's crown of feathers. Because of such internal tension, Panamanian news outlets had reported that journalists were not allowed near the village of the king's palace to investigate the current political topology. I wanted to find out why.

*   *   *

"There is no ban on journalists," said the passenger nimbly seated on the bow of the canoe as we traveled to the Wekso Lodge the night of my arrival. He was curled up in a shoeless ball and was hitching a ride home to a village deeper upstream in the comarca.

Then who was the king? His answer came quickly, as if I should have known. "Tito."

So had the situation returned to normal with Tito back at the helm? Well, not exactly. When I arrived at the lodge, one of the groundskeepers, Milton, an energetic youth who would later educate me on the area's history, asked me what I wanted to do during my time in the kingdom. I responded that I wished to meet the king, if he would be willing to accept me. "You mean you want to meet Valentín?" he asked.

No one at the lodge knew if I'd be able to meet the king— whoever it happened to be—but they would try to arrange a meeting for my last day. During the wait, the lodge wasted no time introducing me to the rest of the centuries-old kingdom that spread out before me along the lush green slopes rising from the River Tjer Di, heard as "Teribe" by the first Spanish explorers. When I told them I enjoyed cooking, I found myself in another dugout canoe (so-called since the canoe is carved out of a single tree trunk) headed across the river to the village of Bonjik, the potential future site of the dam, to help harvest our lunch of palm hearts.

The boat launch of Bonjik, however, looked more like a beach littered with a scattering of dead trees, all curiously facing the same direction—parallel to the river. The Naso territory had withstood its worst flood in 30 years just six weeks before, destroying most of the crops sustaining the village. The disaster stripped the riverbanks raw of all vegetation in a coldly even line 10 feet above the normal level. Were there any palm hearts to harvest?

I followed the squishing rubber boots of Raul, my boatman, leading me to his family's house, its concrete floor offering a respite from the mud and sand smear that was lower Bonjik. Luckily, crops on higher ground survived, which meant that some of the Quintero family's harvests would live to hit the market, including coveted cacao pods and some tender palm shoots like those that would provide our lunch.

His father, Plutarco, a compact bale of calmness in a white t-shirt well soiled from a morning of farming, walked me through what remained of his medicinal plant garden. A monstrous blitzkrieg of water had subjugated the valuable plot into serving as part of the waterway's new riverbed just weeks before and then subsided after taking most of the foliage with it. Protruding oddly from the dead silt, however, a tree crouched, its frame as knurled and stubborn as a centenarian. In a desperate cling, hundreds of worms and other insects hid among its bark.

Plutarco claimed the tree, *viña de bu*, could be prescribed to combat back pain and colic. But he was not alone in realizing its uses; scientists from Western countries such as America and England have offered him $50 for a small, prepared piece. (That might explain the relative fanciness of Plutarco's house with its costly concrete floor.) Still others have paid Plutarco $100 per gallon of an essence made from the bark of another surviving specimen, *caraño ediondo*, utilized for everything from ridding headaches to exorcising evil spirits—not a bad all-around med to keep in the cabinet, for sure. "It's a remedy sent from God," Plutarco remarked.

Playing tug of war with the mud over our footwear, we hiked up an incline to find one of his noni bushes producing knobby, yellow fruit, each covered with dozens of swollen eyes like an embryo gone hideously wrong. But that's just the beginning of the funkiness of this Polynesian transplant. Considering the arresting scent of noni nectar, you might imagine the fruit were paying homage to sun-ripened dumpster juice, yet thrill seekers following the latest in natural remedy trends regularly wince while imbibing a potion of noni juice and milk for the promised yield of sexual power. If the noni works too well, Plutarco can also cook up a remedy for gonorrhea.

In the forest in back of his house, Raul had already found the source of today's palm heart: a pixbae tree. Towering high to steal the sunlight from the runty plants below, the pole of the tree evenly armed its bark with thousands of nasty, 2-inch spines. With a few healthy swings of his machete, Raul hacked off a small shoot growing from its base from which he carved out a femur-sized rod—its heart.

Like many tropical crops, pixbae harbors several uses. Raul would somehow be eluding the tree's thicket of spikes when he harvests its treetop bunches of fruit, peach-sized and tasting somewhere between yucca and chestnuts, in a few weeks when they ripen. I had purchased pixbae fruit before at the markets (where they call the fruit *pifá*) and always boiled them up without knowledge of how they were obtained. Despite the fruit's inexpensiveness at two for a quarter (Panama uses the U.S. dollar as its currency), I grew a new appreciation for pixbae—and especially their farmers.

Meanwhile, Plutarco hacked open a football-sized cacao pod, revealing its cache of slimy white seeds. I found it difficult to imagine that in just one week of fermenting, drying, and roasting, the lathered kernels could morph into that precious substance chocolate, the elixir that had fueled Aztec warriors with battle power and, in our times, provides the trimmings of romance and indulgence. Before me lay its infancy, albino and ugly, cradled in buttery ectoplasm.

And edible, apparently. "Try it, try it," goaded the father and son duo. I dug my fingers into the guts of the pod, my agility matching that of a medical student dunking a clumsy hand into a chest cavity for the first time, until I managed to pluck off a nodule. They both followed my motions with anticipatory concentration as I slid the thing into my mouth. For the briefest of instants, I thought they might have been playing a joke on me but, after a few chews, I began to register a subtle texture redolent of coconut meat, the seed saving a hint of the telltale bitterness of chocolate for its long finish. Pretty tasty. The slime had vindicated itself, yet was still not quite the thing to thrust upon one's sweetheart.

I forgave the seeds again after I drank the creation Raul and his sister had prepared from an already dried batch of cacao seeds back at the house. They had ground up the seeds, then a nutty brown, and mixed them with boiling water and sugar atop their kerosene stove—the only furnishing, besides a radio, lining the plank wall of the house.

I doubted the recipe had been limited just to sugar, water, and cacao seeds, since the viscous drink sprouted with a tingly spice of cinnamon and chili pepper. Too many personalities for too few ingredients. The recipe must have been hiding something else.

"No, just cacao and sugar," Raul laughed, a slightly surprised, slightly apologetic laugh.

Raul had chopped up the palm heart femur—the original objective of the afternoon—and stewed it with onions, garlic cloves, achiote, and chicken consommé. Absent was that bicycle-licking flavor of canned palm hearts; Raul had shown me that fresh palm hearts taste like a tender vegetable, an offering that provided an energetic counterpart to the chocolate libation I had been downing in obsessive haste. I was ready for battle. I was ready for love. "Would you like more?" Raul asked, still laughing at the muffled, Cro-Magnon syllables I had been uttering. Yes, this kingdom was definitely worth defending.

Observing the bouncy faces around the house, I found it easy to forget that the town had been almost completely flushed down the river a few weeks ago. Around Bonjik, people were back in the jungle slashing off fruits and vegetables for their dinners. Seeds were stuffed into the tortured ground. Raul's children snacked on ice cream cones, minus the ice cream—in other words, the cones themselves—a standard snack of the comarca. Girls brushed each other's hair, giggling in a mixture of Spanish and the Naso language, the latter of which pounced upon by scholars because of its rarity and its unusual "prelabialized retroflexed lateral flap phonemes," apparently ear candy for the obsessive linguist yet, to me, I merely heard the undeniable sound of children playing. Only a team of young volunteers from a church group constructing concrete walkways around the town indicated any sense of urgent recovery. The pigs were even happy for a little extra mud in which to romp.

* * *

For every poison dart frog someone had carefully captured in cupped hands for me to see, several more, brought out by the rains, were hunkered down among the undergrowth around the lodge. Barely the width of a quarter, the pretty neon creatures keep themselves off the menu by perfuming their skin with a coating of eau-de-death. Fortunately, their defense is of little threat to a big mammal such as a human, unless someone fancies licking the frogs or spends all afternoon enthusiastically rubbing about a dozen of them into an open wound (to each his own), since the toxin must enter the blood to send its client into paralysis followed by heart failure. Or nothing at all may happen, owing to a few doppelganger species possessing the neon markings but none of the poison with which to back up the threat, although, if I were a groundskeeper, I would have still washed my hands afterward. From intense red to DayGlo camouflage, there were enough varieties to keep a herpetologist crouching on all fours for years — with rubber gloves, I trust.

Junkies aside, at least you can avoid licking a frog. Sometimes, when meandering about the forest, coming face-to-face with a bushmaster snake is unavoidable. That's exactly what happened to Pitino, a lodge groundskeeper and guide, a few days before my arrival. He was clearing a patch of land on which to plant rice when a lounging bushmaster didn't appreciate its jungle home being slashed to bits. One well-placed swing of Pitino's machete cut off the venomous head before it had a chance to deal Pitino a bite boasting a three-in-four mortality rate, and that unsavory statistic includes victims who already received antivenin treatment.

Normally, the rustlings of several people walking would scare away the venomous creatures before they are accidentally stepped on. Three young hiking guides and I, however, were still not able to shake a yellow eyelash viper out of its vigil on a leaf just a foot from a jungle trail on which they took me one morning. The tiny, 18-inch snake held its best pet-like pose — with its exaggerated, cartoon character eyelashes — but I wanted to give the creature its space. I voted that we move on. "It won't attack now. It's not standing up like this," Pitino told me while curling his arm into an S-shaped aggressive posture.

Rosendo, another machete-poking guide leading our pack, remarked, "Don't worry, if it bites you, it won't kill you." It probably will not; the eyelash viper usually leaves its human victim with mere tissue damage or an amputation, depending on where the bite lands. Keep in mind that since the eyelash viper hangs out in trees, bites often occur on the face.

A sting of the bullet ant wouldn't kill anyone either — that is, if there were just one. But these six-legged venom guns, a caravan of which we hopped over, work in a colony of hundreds. After just one sting, however, I would imagine the victim would run away as far as he could, unless he faints from the pain, often described as comparable to a bullet wound, hence the master-of-the-obvious name.

The inherent hazards of a healthy tropical forest do not limit themselves to things that bite, crawl, or jump. Consider the resident mushrooms, for example. Some are tasty. Others are too poisonous even for the most devoted flower child. "Over the generations, we have forgotten which mushrooms are edible, so we stopped picking them," Daniel, an artist and my third guide, narrated as we trekked across the heights of the primary forest, ravines tumbling away on both sides of us. Just last year, he recounted, a Costa Rican living just over the border made a pizza topped with wild mushrooms harvested fresh from the nearby forest. His culinary creativity was rewarded with a road trip to the hospital where he lay on the edge of death for several days before he finally awoke (at which time he swiftly altered his recipe).

Not to be outdone, the recent flood scored a piece of the action when it almost tore down the wooden bridges over the low-lying portion of the trail on which we were walking. One expanse, already weakened with rot, had collapsed on one side, leaving one intact beam across the stream. One at a time, we edged across the good side, clinging to its railing in slow motion, its sole spongy beam ducking with each step. I was glad it wasn't my turn to carry the 40-pound bunch of plantains we had harvested along the way.

When we returned to the lodge, one of the groundskeepers had brought Ana, the cook, a gift of a few quivering scorpions, to try to scare her, I would imagine. He had placed them inside a metal cup that Ana had used before to serve me her guanabana leaf tea. From then on, I always looked into my cup before I drank.

* * *

Almost as unnerving as the destruction caused by the January flood was the timing of the destruction: in the middle of the dry season. Or, at least, January used to be in the middle of the dry season for the region; presently, rain in the comarca arrives year-round without a break. The Nasos blame the recent alteration in climactic temperament on global warming. One villager told me, "Now only soccer has a distinct season here."

The flood felled the lodge's aqueduct, a plastic pipe that used to be tied to a cable above the River Tjer Di. The support posts, along with a segment of the pipe, had long since washed into the Caribbean Sea. Bathing in the outhouse's shower stall became a leisurely scoop-and-pour affair from a 5-gallon bucket, as the occasional voyeur roach, the size of a change purse, watched on.

Another amenity, however, has always been absent: electricity. The impromptu post-dining chats thus fell to the ambience of flashlights and shimmering candles, creating the perfect stage for storytelling time.

"Something bad always happens," Daniel carefully purred from a jack-o-lantern face.   He was recalling recent events concerning a large mountain in the Naso comarca, so tall that "it's always covered in clouds, even when the sun comes out." So tall, in fact, that they don't know exactly how tall it is.

While Nasos regard the earthen behemoth as the Mountain of the Grandmother, many outsiders view the mountain as a money machine, for the old grandmother has hidden gold in her slopes. "I don't know why, but a Latino took gold from her, and he died the next day. There were others who suffered the same fate. If it's not the thief himself, it's a family member of his.   A sickness suddenly and fatally hits. It's a curse. Two or three days after he takes the gold, something bad *always* happens."

In the same moment, a breeze ate the candle's flame. Giant frogs whooped in a spontaneous cacophony from a nearby darkness, heard but not seen. Luckily, I had not planned to go panning for gold.

"We have learned to respect nature," added Pitino from under his upturned sailor's cap, "especially after the flood."

Nature earned my respect, as well, after she gifted me a few entry-level selections from her anthology of tricks. Let us first consider the lodge's oddly chilly nights. At just a few hundred feet above sea level in the tropics, the lodge's elevation falls emphatically short of the heights you would normally associate with wool blankets but, in geographic defiance, the Wekso Lodge courts one's goose bumps at night, owing to the free air conditioning of the fast moving River Tjer Di that gushes past the lodge on two sides. The cold water from the mountains cools the air in a simple interaction the Moors once exploited in some of their Iberian castles, where they cooled the interiors with small troughs of running water, the flow regulated with valves and gravity.   Alas, you cannot switch off the River Tjer Di with a simple closing of a valve.

I even learned a thing or two from some of the smallest residents of the area—leafcutter ants.   One night, the full moon, feeling photogenic, was peeking through a procession of clouds. I wished to set up my mini tripod on a concrete platform left over from the military camp days, but I spotted a highway of leafcutter ants working the graveyard shift.   I stepped over them, setting up the tripod about 10 feet away from their work, and took a few minutes' worth of pictures.

When I was retrieving my camera, I noticed that the ants had changed their route and decided to march right between my crouched legs.   One was trying to gnaw open my boot.   The tiny soldier's hopeless sawing arcs followed a sluggish, contemplative tempo.   It was almost adorable.   After I flicked him off, I noticed about a dozen more on me, including a few on my sock working their way up my pant leg, all following some kind of insidious Tai-Chi march.   Either they were more belligerently territorial than I had thought, or they mistook my legs for trees and they wanted to climb up and harvest whatever dangling fruits they could find.   Neither prospect would do, so I tried to shake them off (bad sideshow act that no one saw), but the determined critters held on.   I had to pick off each one individually, like burrs.

When I walked back to my cabana, I passed my flashlight over myself and checked for any ambitious ants that might have made it up to further elevations.   All clear.   Except the one who had snuck under my briefs, found said fruit, opened jaws, and began to harvest.

*   *   *

Outboard motors have been spewing their syrupy-sweet exhaust along the banks of Naso territory for many years, forever blunting the chore of canoe transport on the Tjer Di. Even now, however, when the rocky knuckles of rapids approach, off goes the motor and out come the push sticks. This hybrid system is the only way to travel against the hurried current of the Tjer Di.

So there I was, the archetypal gringo sitting in the boat between natives doing all the grunt work ("Why, this was how the West was won!" quipped travel writer Tom Miller when in a similar situation). Rather than feeling like a conqueror, I felt more like dead weight, especially when the boat only managed to move a little backwards in the first set of rapids. So with push stick in hand, I was, at last, going to visit the village of the king.

Despite the labor involved, I was still given no guarantees regarding a meeting with the monarch. We just had to show up at Seiyik and hope another coup was not in progress.

But first, I needed to master the dexterity of push-stick operation. The shallowest rapids antagonized the river into frothy ribbons of chaos, some of which ended up in the boat, some of which splashed my push stick fashioned from a stalk of white cane. I failed to realize how slick the pole had become until I dropped it.

The current might have already sucked that stick down to the next village. What would be next? They'll yell at me in Naso. We'll have to back out of the rapids section and dock the canoe near the forest, in search of another piece of white cane to slice up into the right length. The king would be in bed by the time we reached the village. I would attempt to say I was sorry.

While my mind was cultivating the nightmare with diligence, my hand decided to shove itself into the opaque lather behind me. Since the current was darting past us with such fury, I had one chance to grab it. Amidst a blast of water on my arm, I felt a tip of a cane rod smack the palm of my hand as if a relay runner had expertly passed me a baton. And, thus, I received my first—and only—real-world payoff for lettering in high school track.

Once we reached a smooth stretch, Raul dipped the motor back into the river. Rafts, tied together with fibers found in the jungle, gingerly floated past us downstream. At first, the two or three huddled standees atop each tiny raft appeared as desperate escapees from a shipwreck but, in fact, they deftly controlled the raft by pushing cane sticks into the water for steering. They even raised plenty of spare arms to wave at us. While rafts form a popular mode of transportation along the Tjer Di, they have one limitation: owing to the rushed current, they can only be used for traveling downstream.   But in the Naso comarca, little goes to waste. Once the rafts reach the launch port downstream at El Silencio, the wood is promptly collected and used for constructing houses.

After over an hour of ducking under low boughs and poking through rapids, we arrived at Seiyik, home of the king. The village was also the home of Leonardo, the other boatman, who lived on the other side of the village. We would lunch there at a nearby friend's elevated pole house to avoid meeting a monarch on an empty stomach.

En route to our midday meal, Leonardo utilized our hiking to introduce me to some of the techniques of Naso agriculture. He walked me through his meandering plot of knobby cacao trees, their pods dangling from the trunks and branches like punching bags. While some pods succumbed to fungal infections, turning the pods from a healthy yellow or burgundy into a nasty black— sometimes with frosty white splotches—a scourge that has turned many Panamanian farmers away from growing cacao, Leonardo remained indifferent as we passed the damaged fruit. Unlike the commercial cacao growers who planted their trees close together and lost most or all of their crops to fungus, despite using potent fungicides, Leonardo's organically grown trees were still yielding a comfortable majority of pods that were healthy and ready to be harvested. (Scientists have recently demonstrated that a particular fungus that grows on cacao trees actually repels the more harmful fungi, similar to how hiring a Moroccan souk guide keeps away the others.)

He regularly sells the cacao, more valuable since it's organic, to a cooperative that markets it to American and European companies. Panama's cacao exports, compared with other cacao growing countries, remain miniscule—500 metric tons per year—barely enough to make a bar of chocolate for each Panamanian. That's only about one ten-thousandth of the world's yearly chocolate haul. In other words, you have a better chance of dying in a car accident than encountering a bar of Panamanian chocolate outside of Panama (sorry about that). But to the Naso, the trickle of income provides real money and is the only proof they need to remain organic.

Other Naso farmers I had met also boasted fortune in growing crops year after year, while many farmers in other parts of Panama struggle to squeeze a few successful years out of a slash-and-burn plot. Slashing-and-burning means cutting all vegetation with a machete and then burning it to concentrate the soil's nutrients in preparation for seeding, providing a fat crop in the first year. Unfortunately, the burning kills off the microbes and fungi necessary to rejuvenate the nutrients and general health of the soil, rendering the soil poor in just a few years.

In contrast, the Naso slash, but they don't burn. That, they claim, is a factor in the health of their soil. Whether planting rice, plantains, chili peppers, or cacao, the Naso farmers leave dead vegetation—discarded cacao pods included—on the ground around the crops as a pig-out for the microbes and fungi, in turn keeping the soil nutrient-high. No chemicals are needed.

But the Naso farmers have stocked more tricks up their soil-smeared sleeves.   An avoidance of large swatches of monoculture — most families tend their own individual plots, often mixing crops together — maintains biodiversity of the land, a move further enriching the quality of the soil. Add to that the use of organic fertilizer, like dead vegetation, and you have maximized the use of tropical soil, the soil that bears a bad name for being difficult to tease into commercial use. After all, how can soil that supports some of the lushest vegetation on the planet be considered poor? The answer seems to depend on how it is used.

"The soil here is very fertile," Leonardo commented, uttering a statement I have rarely heard in the tropics.

Nothing illustrated the point better than the plantain trees that had been planted into the apparent wasteland created by the flood.   Farmers simply dug into the layer of useless sand deposited by the flood to reach the topsoil and planted the seeds. In a month, the plantain sprouts had not only pushed their way up through the sand, but had also peered more than a foot above ground. On a riverbank of Seiyik, Leonardo and I dug into the new beach to discern its depth and discovered that the flood had coated the bank with 4 inches of sand, apparently no match for the determined bud of a plantain tree — a fitting metaphor for the resolve of the Naso themselves.

That is not to say that all matters agrarian had reverted back to normalcy in the Naso community. Seeds were still scarce, and the government had limited flood relief support to a supply of food lasting only a few days. It was up to the families to acquire the seeds they needed, with what income they could cull, from the sales of other crops still standing. Artisans set up makeshift stores on their porches to sell cedar crafts (including ceremonial spears resembling the king's very own) to the occasional visitor — occasional indeed: except for a missionary translating his bible into the Naso language, I was the only other outsider inside the comarca at the time.

For additional income, some cooks employed their traditional talents, as was the case with our lunch. Atop a pole house overlooking a cloud-numbed river valley, the two guides and I put away bowls of rice topped with a stew of *ñame*, a starchy root vegetable, and pink chunks of elusively anonymous animal protein: Panama's very own Spam knockoff. Raul called it "poor man's meat." And that's not even counting the dollop of monkey's tail.

But before you think we have left a simian crawling around the forest floor, one dexterous appendage short, *rabo de mono*, or monkey's tail, is a green plant whose tender tip, which curls in a spiral, is plucked off just before mealtime. While the *rabo de mono*, a Naso favorite, softly crunched like the dark greens they were, a sinister richness pervaded, too carnivorous for a vegetable. No doubt, the cook had stewed them in a meat broth?

Raul laughed at me again from the lull of a swaying hammock. "No, just *rabo de mono* and salt."

I could only conclude that a Naso farmer, possibly after eating the wrong mushrooms, had somehow crossbred a mountain pig with broccoli rabe, either by accident or by design, creating some self-grazing miracle of photosynthesis. At the least, I wanted to learn the name of the bakery/restaurant/store. Despite the nutritive commerce within, the pole house was as unmarked as the others in the village, the locale only indicating its trade with an open, shelved window, a trait I had come to recognize in some of the more rural hamlets in Panama. Still, the neighbors must call it *something*, whether it sits under a buzzing 5000-watt neon sign or not.

When I asked Leonardo, he froze the start of a mischievous grin and, in a moment, answered, "Breezes in the Middle of the Night." We had a good laugh. It was as good a name as any.

Before we left, I needed to visit Breezes in the Middle of the Night's outside facilities. I lifted off the piece of wood serving as the door of the outhouse to find the room occupied by an iguana perched on the rim of the wall, overlooking the depths of the seatless seat. We gave each other the same perplexed and vaguely horrified stare that asked, "What are *you* doing here?"

* * *

The location of the king's palace had been chosen prudently, since to approach, you need to follow a path up an abrupt slope that discourages passage with mud slime guarding every earthen step. I just imagined the difficulties encountered by the Bribri, a nearby indigenous nation and historical enemy of the Naso, during one of their skirmishes. The top of the path was easily defendable, since invaders had to climb up the spindly route from the river single file.

Then again, the Naso reckoned with their own wartime disadvantages, for the Naso wore openly-visible incandescent paint, derived from a jungle plant, on their bodies into battle, while the Bribri warriors went as dark as the night, fighting only with the power of *sukias*, or witch doctors, as the story had been conveyed to me by Pitino back at the lodge.

The peculiar stakes of the game kept the two tribes at war for centuries, for the victors would carry off the women as prizes — making war to make love. Perhaps given the eventual mixing of the bloodlines between the two rival tribes due to the nature of the spoils, their period of aggression has come to an end. Now, when a Naso wants to marry a Bribri, they skip the war part and just make love.

While I had entered the comarca at a time of inter-tribal peace, the Naso's internal political climate remained heated. I was informed that the royal flavor of the month was Valentín, the uncle, who was working in his modest office when we arrived. I had also gathered information that in addition to Seiyik, six more of the 11 Naso villages stood by Valentín, with the remaining four, including Bonjik — the future site of the dam project — supporting Tito, the nephew. While Tito was busy attempting to instrument laws for the kingdom at a Panamanian town located outside the roadless comarca, Valentín was busy firming up his own base of followers inside.

With Leonardo, I stood outside the administrative building that doubled as the royal palace, an unimposing structure of zinc roofing and cinder blocks that resembled a rural Panamanian school more than the seat of government, yet within its cozy catacombs lay the king's office, the royal family's home, and, just a few walls over, the comarca's jail. At least criminals don't have too far to walk to grovel for forgiveness.

After waiting days and traveling up the rapids, would I be able to speak with the monarch? Messengers were sent in. They emerged with word that in light of recent events, the king was very busy, and I should not count on a meeting. Go-betweens shuffled back and forth. An afternoon rain arrived. Negotiations continued.

With promise of taking the king's story to print, I scored a few minutes with the month-old king. An entourage of his supporters escorted me through barracks-inspired rooms until we entered a vestibule jammed with two-dozen men circling a desk, behind which hid a tiny, tranquil man. To me, he shifted his eyes, soft yet investigative, and topped his head with his newly acquired crown of feathers, bringing him more formality than pleasure. The room turned to me and hushed.

I realized just then that I had not a clue about how to greet the king, since I had never greeted a king before. Should I kneel, salute, or just shake his hand? What do I say first?

Congratulations on your successful coup?   And I wondered if I were wearing appropriate attire. My hiking boots were plastered with mud, like bonbons for Godzilla.   So the first thing plummeting from my tongue was an apology for my appearance.

The king didn't respond right away. Since he only spoke the Naso language, he waited for one of his cabinet members to translate from the Spanish. Giggles burbled about. "The king says not to worry because mud pretty much goes with the territory around here."

I accepted his answer as a signal of approval and began attempting to uncover what many journalists had supposedly failed to.   As I discovered, however, the king served as more of a spiritual eminence than a micromanager.   In reference to my inquiry about the specifics of the dam project, Valentín, in a soothing croak, expounded about how the dam would only succeed in damaging collective Naso land—and the environment—all while fulfilling his nephew's personal monetary ends, more or less what I had already been told by others.

The new designation of the Naso comarca, an indigenous territory inside the Panamanian province of Bocas del Toro, assigned the law of the king as the law of the comarca, after 30 years of struggle with Panama for recognition. Yet he chose not to mention the taxes still levied on the Naso by Panama. Since most of the comarca lies inside national park territory, the Naso still pay taxes on everything from slaughtering a pig to felling a tree. The king was not even able to assist in securing me a map of the comarca's boundaries, since his nephew ran off with the only good map he knew of.

Details mattered not; as he glowed in a timid luminescence, a few breaths of his dialogue (strengthened by the commanding power of those "prelabialized retroflexed lateral flap phonemes," I think) had duly seized the attention of the gathering, dozens of rubber boots pointing towards the desk in silence. He was their champion; his interests swam with his agrarian subjects; he toiled in a featureless cell, instead of a lavish palace. Even learning Spanish, a skill necessary to shake and shimmy with the politicians of Panama City, seemed less important to him than defending the traditions of the Naso. Seven generations of monarchs from the Santana family had not led their people into selling out their culture to the worship of cash.

Or did they? The translator turned to me after I asked my last question. "In return for the king's time," he remarked with the polite urgency a patient master employs to correct a novice in training, "a gesture of a little 'incentive' would be appreciated."

Shame on me for being such an uncouth guest. I had shown up at the door of the king without a gift! I still had one option: the universal present.

"How much is a little?" I asked. The office wobbled with laughter. While haggling is a requisite step in the ballet of many Panamanian transactions, I suddenly felt that haggling with the king of the Naso might have been crossing the line. I left a few greenbacks on his desk with a careful smile, which was returned by a slow, warm nod of his crown of feathers. Perhaps not all 'incentives' lead to selling out.

* * *

The meeting was reason to celebrate. Ana had been preparing the celebration in the lodge's kitchen, blending ingredients grown nearby. Those very edible prizes were what the Naso's tradition of small-plot agriculture delivers, the same prizes that the king Valentín has claimed he will defend.

For my last dinner at Wekso, Ana, once again, employed versatility with the fewest of local provisions, chalking up yet another use for *ñame*—a tuber we had almost tripped over a few times on our hikes — slicing it very thinly and frying it into chips. She flanked them with creamy wedges of avocado.   Sweet pineapple, obscenely juicy, had arrived from Seiyik; the bread came from another's unmarked pole house; and the tea from leaves Ana picked off fruit trees around the lodge.   A farmer from Bonjik had rounded up a plump bag of *rabo de mono* and handed it to us in the canoe on the way back from Seiyik, providing a foundation of rich meat to the meal, minus the meat — quite a switch from the caveman's carpaccio served here to Noriega's graduating soldiers 16 years ago.

It was a meal suitable for a king. Or maybe two.

Author's note: a month after my departure, a comarca-wide vote crowned Tito as monarch of the Naso once again. Valentín's supporters boycotted the vote due to what they viewed as a corrupt election process that bowed to interference from outside the comarca.

2.
186,000 Chickens

THE DRY SEASON WINDS love El Valle in a simple-minded, golem-kind of way. I permanently employed a hand to secure my straw hat to my head, but the campesinos of the miniature plain didn't need to resort to such inefficiency. With so many crops to usher along and so much tropical sun to deflect, the farmers reserved both hands for their livelihood while the rims of their hats clung defiantly to their foreheads in a charming defeat of the laws of aerodynamics.

Such talent doesn't seem to be the first thing recalled when El Valle is mentioned, however. A little over two hours from Panama City resides a mountain-ringed town inside an extinct volcano, better known by *capitaleños* (folks from the capital) as well as tourists for its crafts market on Sundays. Since I arrived on a Saturday, the valley was still savoring a siesta. The napping dogs on Avenida Central didn't even bother to look up when my girlfriend Melanie and I emerged from the bowels of the public bus.

Only the most casual drip of commerce rode out the afternoon, the town modestly drawing in a deep breath before its weekly notoriety struck. Campesinos began to return from planting seeds in the fields. Piles of fried chicken sat uneaten under bare bulbs. In a meditative dress rehearsal, the owner of an everything-for-a-quarter table reclined behind his wares and spared his announcement voice for the next day. A few children chatted in a stall of watermelons and coconuts, the rim of the stall's zinc roof adorned with torso-sized bunches of pixbae (a popular fruit with a flavor somewhere between a potato and a chestnut). Only the wind from the north refused to join the town's repose—and the floorboards of our two-story hotel replied to the wind with a peaceful creaking, like an old schooner.

In the evening, however, the town stripped off its dreamy husk. A stereo bursting with salsa—accompanied by a live, amplified female vocalist—had, at once, commandeered the parking lot in front of the hotel. Since the town so thoughtfully brought Saturday night revelry to the doorstep of its guests, I walked outside and decided to join the festivities.

But what breed of festivity had I happened upon? A tight circle of teens were chanting and clapping—a pulsing millipede of polyester and puberty. In the center, instead of a pair indulging the crowd with a demonstration of slick footwork, some dancers, who had mislaid the tempo, began collapsing onto the lot. They remained motionless. As I began to understand the vocalist, who kept showering the gathering in the rhythm of an auctioneer, I realized that I had walked into a celebration in the name of Christianity.

Then the tape stopped. The tambourine tapered off its last jingle and the millipede began to dissolve about the lot. Those on the ground began to carefully rise back up, energized faces emerging.

I approached a parishioner in a lightweight blazer and a vigorous smirk. I asked him what the occasion was. His group had traveled six hours from the western province of Chiriquí and selected El Valle as a target for their traveling bonanza of evangelicalism.

"I'm staying in a room just upstairs from the lot and was curious to see what was happening," I commented.

He nodded proudly. His laughter broke into a cackle when I told him I had been just about to sleep.

"Why did the people fall?" I asked, simultaneously pandering to my curiosity and his glory.

"*El espíritu santo.*" The Holy Spirit.

It was interesting how the Holy Spirit had ripped me out of bed while, at the same time, placing the parishioners gently on the ground to rest. I suppose such preferential treatment is a members-only perk. The man handed me a small booklet emblazoned with the name of their church, so if I wanted, I, too, could fall into trances along the Pan-American Highway. The troupe squeezed itself into their van and left in search of another stage and another audience.

Aside from the brief whistle-stop of the Holy Spirit, the valley settled into silence until the arrival of rental cars filled with foreign tourists and buses filled with *capitaleños* in the morning. The covered market area soon bulged with an orgy of colorful dyed baskets, potted flowers, hovering Bermuda shorts, and carvings painted with the word PANAMA. "*Todo la cuara, todo la cuara,*" barked the 25-cent table man, employing Panama's smooth bastardization of "quarter" in an attempt to shake shoppers free from other tables' hand-carved souvenirs and toward his array of pens, crude padlocks, and plastic toys. Capitalizing on the geyser of vacation money, a few Kuna arrived selling molas, albeit, at a markup from what you may negotiate for the reverse-appliqué works in the Caribbean islands of Kuna Yala.

Several vendors sold edible items, toward which the *capitaleños* tended to gravitate. For 50 cents, a refreshing coconut could be "machete-d" open and a straw stuffed inside. Considering it was the end of March, the booty of cashew season had arrived in dollar bags, their contents toasted and still a little chewy. Only the *raspado*, the flavored ice bike, hauled in as many *cuaras* as the vendor selling caramel in shallow paper cups, the cups' lids serving as makeshift spoons.

Live chickens passed down Avenida Central in the hands of *valleros*, some carrying them like footballs, others dangling them upside down. According to Panama's Office of Statistics and Census, which also counts livestock, there are 30 chickens for each of El Valle's 6,200 residents, not counting their deep-fried afterlives that still sat patiently under a purgatory of hot bulbs.

While American tourists were busy trying to make the clay artwork vendors understand English, the town's only museum was open during its only hours of the week—Sunday from 10 a.m. until 2 p.m. Since Melanie and I represented the sole visiting party to the garage-sized museum for the day, the guide took his time showing us the museum's very own sculpture of Jesus as a *mestizo*—that is, of mixed Amerindian and European descent—yet another tome from the worldwide compendium of ethnic Jesi.

His other item that received an endearingly long-winded narration was a stone carved with ornate petroglyphs, said to depict the worshipping of a god from a pre-Columbian culture. But not everyone has interpreted the stone's markings the same way. Years ago, the squared-off boulder was discovered in the ground by a grandmother of the town who, apparently, found the grooves of the chiseled glyph handy for washing clothes. When existence of the treasure was brought to the attention of historians, it was moved to the museum (by that time, I would imagine it required little cleaning).

The gift shop consisted entirely of a book on El Valle, bound with rusty staples and written by the priest of the museum's adjacent church. Extracting an astonishing amount of history from such a petite valley, the meticulous Father José Noto has covered everything from the valley's ancient geological temperament to an old El Valle witch doctor's remedy for a headache that lists rum as its main ingredient.

The end of the dry months in El Valle also signaled the harvest of tangerines from the mountain fincas surrounding the town. On a footpath to the valley's largest petroglyph, a team of tangerine pickers bounded down the stone and dirt trail barefoot, each burdened with a *motete* — a barrel-sized basket strapped to the back — filled with tangerines. Forcefully puffing air in and out, the citrus pickers dove around hikers and nursing mothers alike, the flesh of their feet instinctively missing the occasional sharp rocks lying in wait along the path.

The grooves of the petroglyph, called La Piedra Pintada — the painted stone — bear an almost Picasso-esque geometry, yet extracting their original meaning is about as subjective as superimposing human-centric shapes over star clusters. Spanning 8 meters in width and 4 in height — too large and too vertical on which to conveniently wash clothes — the wall of chiseled doodlings may just as well prove to be graffiti of an unknown age. In fact, the word *"pintada"* also happens to mean "graffiti" in Spanish. Perhaps the ambiguous name has doomed the fate of the rock; some modern graffiti wannabes couldn't help themselves and recently spray-painted a few boneheaded words in Spanish over the glyphs.

Back in town, but away from the market, the town seemed as it did the day before, having no need for donning a guidebook sidebar façade. Kids made a game out of collecting bottles from a drainage gutter right below a "Please don't litter" sign. Dogs extended their siestas. The bulbs above the fried chicken were working hard. Regular-sized bicycles wobbled along Avenida Central carrying their usual two — sometimes three — passengers. An American school bus, now reincarnated as Panamanian public transportation, moaned over its route to the village of La Pintada and back. Its rear door blessed the town with a painted Jesus sporting a flattering yellow halo between the bus' dual exhaust pipes.

And the oafish wind from the north refused to relent. But there was reason to take delight. If the wind comes from the north, as any *vallero* will tell you, it will not rain. If it comes from the south, then all bets are off. Regardless of direction, however, the raw power of the gusts across the area must be respected, for just the day before, according to the daily *La Critica*, a man was blown to his death from the top of a radio tower in Chorrera, a nearby town to the east.

* * *

After the caravan of basket-filled rental cars had returned to Panama City, El Valle surrendered itself to a peaceful namelessness. The entrance to the bar Jardín Bambú cast a slumbering light over Avenida Central. Instead of a door, the concrete structure only claimed a wall in front of its opening, similar to what you might find in front of a latrine to allow ventilation. When we entered, I realized that permanent ventilation was not a bad idea.

NO BAR TABS read a hand-painted sign. The bar's patrons were sparsely seated along the interior's perimeter like remaining teeth in a mouth ravaged by decay. Dirty bulbs glazed the room with jaundice. Against the wall, the jukebox stood glittering, yet alone and quiet, like a prostitute on a slow night. Heads lay serenely motionless, buried into the counter. I thought I had become stuck in the grooves of a skipping Tom Waits song minus the piano.

I was only a few sips into my 50-cent bottle of Atlas beer when a figure peeled itself from the counter. His uncooperative legs thrashed towards us and sat down at our table. The young face, copper and grinning, studied mine for an instant.

"Mi pais es su pais," he announced with swirling gestures. *My country is your country.* A day laborer from the valley, he said he wanted to make sure we were enjoying ourselves in Panama. When I mentioned that we lived abroad, he tilted his head back. "I was once in love with a beautiful woman from Spain, but she didn't love me back," he said through a reclined, frozen smile, as if he were retelling a sweet memory. "It's because I'm an Indian."

His manual punctuation had grown so intense that he knocked over my beer, adding a fresh layer of slime to the table. No problem, I'll just get another one, I thought. But he waved away my wallet and beckoned for the waitress. His arm swings became grander with each "no, allow me" I volleyed toward him.

When, at last, I slumped back in concession to his offer, his smile returned. *"Mi pais es su pais."*

After hearing the story of cross-continental unrequited love again, my new bottle was half down. He wanted to buy me another, but we felt we should leave before he had the chance, for if he were earning the average Panamanian farm labor wage of $7 a day, I did not want be responsible for helping it disappear. He shook my hand in a big, beefy arc. "Don't forget, *mi pais es su pais.*"

It was midnight along Avenida Central and foot traffic was reduced to a rarity. But a lone generator still murmured from a roadside stall, familiar bulbs simultaneously lighting the way and keeping the town snack warm. The market had packed up, the Holy Spirit had moved on, wages had been drunk away, even the wind, at last, had taken a break—leaving an ability to manage circumstances that, like fried chicken, remained in an unfailing supply.

3.
Voting for Garbage
Is Prohibited

THE PANAMA CANAL is usually regarded in terms of traveling through it, but Panamanians, whose country has been neatly sliced in two, more often need to cross over it. For the latter purpose, 200,000 passengers per day utilize the photogenic Bridge of the Americas, connecting the Pacific sides of the country with its inchworm-shaped span suspending the roadway 201 feet above high tide.

But what about crossing over the Canal at other places further north? Another bridge is being built further inland, but has garnered its nickname of the "Bridge to Nowhere," due to its stalled construction.

That leaves a third possibility. The Atlantic-side swing bridge, the only alternate passage currently available to land vehicles, just takes a little patience.

At sea level, I waited in an idling 4x4 taxi for a fleeting chance to cross the aforementioned span that would swing across the Canal leading to the western part of the Colón province. While Panama graces vehicles with opportunities to wait for the crossing of goats, ducks, and even giant frogs, the swing bridge is the only place where cars yield to 40,000-ton cargo ships.

When would the light turn green? "Sometimes 15 minutes, sometimes hours," answered Eric Jackson, editor of *The Panama News*, who accompanied me for the journey. Eric, raised in what used to be the American-administered Canal Zone, was speaking from his experiences living near the city of Colón. The driver, Dumas, took his cue from the red light to snack on a fruit salad to pass the time. Other drivers in line left their vehicles, leaning on quarter panels and nodding into cell phones.

But the drivers dared not stray too far from their cars. Once the light turned green — which happened with no warning — half-eaten apples were tossed, curses flew, and doors failed to close properly as the queue gunned onto the tiny bridge, freshly moved into place a few giddy feet above the Atlantic tide. To the right, a 100-foot wide cargo vessel, safely tethered to trains alongside the Canal, poked its steely snout above the taxi. The intersection was not one conducive to running red lights.

We had entered the half of the province named Costa Abajo, or "lower coast," referring to how the coast gradually falls away from the city of Colón. Why hire a 4x4? Pavement remains a cruel fantasy the further you travel out into Costa Abajo. To make matters worse, the dry season had thus far proven rather wet. Our mission was to reach as far west along the coast as Dumas' pickup would take us.

The first few miles into Costa Abajo used to be inside the Canal Zone, its paved calmness providing no confrontation for Dumas' truck. We followed the sweeping curves leading to the spillway of the Gatun Dam, a deceivingly small structure for hemming in the 85-foot high waterline of the manmade Gatun Lake. But the spillway only represents the most ostentatious cog of the engineering work. The smooth arcs of shaped terrain surrounding the spillway form an earthen dam more than a mile long, to which Eric referred as quite the setting for a future amphitheater. I could just imagine how such ample space could be utilized as a venue for Macbeth's killing spree or, better yet, for fleshing out the drama of how the Gatun Dam came close to never being built.   In retrospect, the graceful structure appears as fittingly necessary to the Canal as citrus juice to ceviche.   But when a French company began digging the Canal in 1880, the project's fundraiser and coordinator, Ferdinand de Lesseps, didn't even have plans for a dam at Gatun.   He had just finished impressing the world with his clean-cut Suez Canal through Egypt and, for his next trick, he would blast a clean-cut, sea-level canal through the continental divide of Panama.

But the euphoria from the Suez feat had clouded early blunders in the new canal's planning.   De Lesseps, a diplomat, ignored the advice of an engineer and fellow countryman, Adolphe Godin de Lépinay, who prophesized that the sea-level canal project was plagued with geographical headaches.   The engineer, instead, favored a lock-based canal approach that would form an artificial lake and require a large dam at Gatun.   While the digging across the continental divide fell victim to endless landslides and the deaths of an estimated 20,000 workers, mostly from malaria and yellow fever, de Lesseps' company buckled under a landslide of corruption.

By the time de Lesseps decided to switch to a lock-based approach, which required much less digging, since the locks would raise boats above most of the continental divide, the remaining funds had been diverted into the pockets of blackmailers and away from French investors.   Many of the latter lost their life savings.

While the canal digging continued at a numbed pace under a new half-spirited French company, a *National Geographic* article from 1889—the magazine's first volume—declared, "The canal will remain, as it is now, the most gigantic failure of the age."

Enter a squad of walrus-mustached politicians and lawyers who smelled monetary opportunity above the carrion. The lobbyers began goading American congress to drop the planned canal project through Nicaragua and, instead, snap up a bargain handyman special: the partially dug trench through Panama, then a province of Colombia. The only catch: to secure the closeout sale price of $40 million, America had to use her persuasion to assist the seceding of independence-hungry Panama from Colombia, or else pay a higher price to Colombia and receive fewer lease amenities. Reversing an all-but-done deal to start digging across the flatter Nicaragua route, the lobbyists for the isthmian canal stole away the senate's confidence. The dream of parting the isthmus once again seized the front pages of world newspapers.

But when the American government bought the canal interest from the new French company in 1903 — midwifing the sovereign country of Panama in the process — the first American engineers, armed with advances in the steam shovel technology of the past decade and an infusion of cowboy hubris, ignored the failure of the French company's attempt. The Americans still desired to resume cutting a clean, sea-level canal through the isthmus. The digging continued without direction — literally. A rustling of critics began to contemplate alternate canal routes.

Once again, the ditch refused to become its own grave. Engineering turnover revived the project when Theodore Roosevelt appointed the self-taught, railroad champion John F. Stevens as the new chief engineer. Stevens promptly raided the original plan proposed by shunned engineer de Lépinay from almost 30 years earlier and reverted the blueprint back to a lock-based canal, complete with a dam at Gatun and enhancements such as wider locks to accommodate America's latest battleships.

It wasn't too long before *National Geographic* hopped back on board and declared that the impending completion of the Canal "will live through all the ages as the greatest single monument to human energy." The Canal opened, at last, for business in 1914, just in time to be eclipsed by the first volleys of World War I.

But such a complex, gargantuan creation seems to have been sentenced to a future of complex, gargantuan attention. Aside from the natural adversaries such as landslides, the Canal has been perceived, periodically, as a target—from World War II to present day terrorism—although one of the more curious threats emerged from within Panama. In 1977, when the Canal and the former Canal Zone were still administered by the United States, Panama's famously benevolent dictator Omar Torrijos—so benevolent that bus drivers still paint his cigar-puffing likeness onto their buses—confided in writer Graham Greene that if the negotiations to hand over the Canal Zone to Panama had soured, Torrijos would have bombed Gatun Dam. The dictator believed that the damage would have lowered the water level of Gatun Lake such that three years would be required to raise it back up, ending all Canal traffic and the America-bound income derived from it during such time, whilst the Panamanian military would disappear into the jungle and nurture a Vietnam-style guerrilla war.

Such a romantic maneuver might have never succeeded anyway, since the Americans had contingency plans for repairing the spillway, and an ordinary bomb dropped on the 8,200-foot earthen dam would have created, as Eric was quick to suggest, little more than "a lake for raising some tilapia."

Fish was on my mind as we approached the towns of Costa Abajo in search of a restaurant, even though the only recent guidebook of the country had stated that there were none in the entirety of the region. We decided to gamble with our hunger and proceed anyway. Game abounded in the jungle around the Canal, but hunting would be foolish, not by reason of flaunting environmental laws (with the country's limited budget for ecological pursuits, it is rare that poachers ever get caught). A more salient deterrent was that much of the area's forest used to serve as an American firing range and remains sprinkled with live ordnance. Panama claims that unexploded rounds have taken the lives of 21 of her citizens working as guards at the bases or collecting scrap metal for recycling, although the United States maintains that the confirmed toll remains at seven.

Passing through Achiote, a farming town with speed bumps instead of traffic lights, we stopped at the flotsam-strewn beaches of Piña on the Caribbean Sea, where a few grinning youngsters on a front porch greeted us with a display of their roosters raised for fighting. Farming and cattle ranching provide income for the Piñans nowadays, although much of the inland area used to be a Dutch-owned palm plantation that grew a species far from the postcard-ready, supple varieties slung with hammocks; rather, the plantation cultivated stocky, unattractive palm trees for its oil. A wealth of the former variety, however, sprouts along the coastal stretches of the road, sans hammocks. A real estate investor might view the beautifully desolate waterfront property as underdeveloped, since the area's beach had attracted scarcely more than a few machete-swinging coconut harvesters and a hand-painted sign lettered with PROHIBIDO VOTAR BASURA, or "voting for garbage is prohibited." Either the Piñans can't spell very well—writing *votar* (to vote for) instead of *botar* (to throw out)—or they are still passionately celebrating Panama's 1990 return to democracy after over 20 years of military rule.

Except for a few tufts of cracked blacktop left over from the era of the Dutch palm oil venture, the road carried on without pavement. A team of barefooted men helped themselves to shovels full of the beach's sand—a raw material for making concrete—which the group chucked into a truck bed older than they were.

Carcasses of once-colorful *diablos rojos*—Panamanian public buses—rusted and faded peacefully along the Martian dirt of the road. The sight of the metal beasts laid to rest is, in fact, telling of the general inaccessibility of the area, especially when you consider that scrap metal recycling has become the latest craze on the isthmus. In addition to the harvesting of usual roadside junk, the disciples of the frenzy have been excitedly hacking off parts of working factory machines, and even bridges, for a quick buck. But judging from the integrity of the detritus we kept passing, it seems as if *fiebre del hierro*, or iron fever, as one newspaper has christened the fad, has not yet infected the tranquil neglect of Costa Abajo.

Speaking of *diablos rojos*, the path proved little challenge for those buses still running. Their graffiti-inspired paint jobs splashed a periodic passing of sun-lightened color upon the fields of pasture, as thick stalks of dead palm trees—all that remained of them—poked up from the grass like ruins of awkward roman pillars, horses casually grazing around them.

The road grew sludgy around the time wooden crosses along the road—the standard Latin American markings of the sites of horrific traffic accidents—began appearing with sobering frequency. As if the patches of mud were not sufficient deterrents against driving like a lunatic, the village decided to construct earthen speed bumps to avoid having to stake down another cross. We crept slowly.

The easy pace wound up our hunger, just in time for our discovery of a restaurant at Boca de Rio Indio. As children treated beach-combing vultures as playmates, anglers were busy scooping up nets full of jurel, snapper, and shad at the river's mouth, providing one of the fresh offerings to be fried at the multitasking Restaurante Nani. Inside the structure, which also served as a grocery kiosk and someone's house, we straddled stools tacked with linoleum. Nani's proved that there was, luckily, a place to eat in Costa Abajo without having to grow/spear/catch lunch yourself. I could not finish the starchy overload of my order of *patacones* (slices of fried green plantains), so I gave them to Dumas for a snack to go. They would come in handy later.

"You can't go much farther than here," the fishermen from the village told us. "The road becomes impassable after a few miles." But buses were still carefully proceeding westward. So we would too.

Not all buses returned, however. Another *diablo rojo* carcass sat at the beach's edge like a bather coyly testing the water. "If this bus were just 100 meters out to sea," Eric stated into the salty breeze, "you'd have a coral reef."

Dumas cared not to donate his truck as a potential home for tropical fish, so he switched to four-wheel drive. The route grew wet and sparse, overlooked by an unkempt palm oil tree here, a broken bulldozer-turned-flowerpot there. Smoothly bobbing down the road, a horse carried a jug of kerosene on its side, the animal ironically providing the transportation lifeline for some distant machine, instead of vice versa. Ravines had eaten up half the road, the other half ready for a motocross race. Dumas snared a *patacon* from the takeout container. "For strength," he mumbled between chews, "in case we have to get out and push."

We soon hit the western limit of bus service. But rare is a road in Panama, paved or otherwise, that is not prowled regularly with some kind of collective transport. Where we were driving, any four-wheel drive vehicle passing by served as the bus' replacement. Passengers waiting at "stops" (although anywhere along the road seemed fine) would hop in the back of the pickups, standing for the ride, along with whatever cargo the truck had been toting, and would rap on the roof of the truck to tell the driver where to drop them off.

"Mama," whimpered Dumas as the tires slurped through the pudding of the highway. At particularly bothersome stretches where the road disappeared into mire of questionable depth, trucks in the days before us had driven around the mess and carved new routes alongside them. Dumas grimaced as his truck did its part to help form the new passages. "Papa!"

We entered and left the town of Gobea, whose downtown consists wholly of a cockfighting palace. The route headed to the beach for a few bends, the sand providing a much smoother ride, save the tender chafe of sea grape leaves against the doors. Chickens fussed about the shaded sand. We stopped so that I could procure coconut juice from a harvester sitting on a rock next to a pile of his bounty. After the coconut man played the how-much-you-want/how-much-you-got game with me, I enjoyed my overpriced, but fresh, coconut juice, which I swigged right out of the husk.

Back inland, the naughty mud path waited in ambush. Dumas resorted to pleading with a generation older. "Grandma!" he cried, stifling his unease with a *patacon*.

With the full force of Dumas' family spirits carrying us through, we followed the trail snaking through jungle until we approached a clearing. We were happening upon Miguel de la Borda, the last town reachable by land vehicle. What secrets, romantic or wicked, would the extreme end of an extreme passage thrust upon us?

Well, Miguel de la Borda turned out to be another zinc-roofed Panamanian town with a charmingly small square and obligatory church. Contemplative horses stood tethered to posts under palm trees. Dumas crept forward until the road met its unceremonious, but definitive, terminus in front of a bench populated with folks staring at the roving dirt-cake approaching them. We had made it to the end of the road. And we were still squarely in Panama.

While Eric assumed his journalistic duties and found conversation with the villagers about a controversial mining concession that would affect the area, three girls who were sitting on the bench sequestered me to take their picture on the town's new pier, a shining enclave of infrastructure bankrolled with aid from international organizations.

With no post office and no Internet, the girls lived in a village four mired hours from the city of Colón (in the dry season), yet they modeled the latest figure-hugging fashion of the urbanite so well, as to strike envy in the hips of martini-fed Panama City club hoppers. Evidently, television comes in clearly in Miguel de la Borda.

For additional recreation, the ranching and fishing town boasted a billiard hall larger than their judge's office. They had a choice of three Chinese-run grocery stores in which to hang out and hide from the afternoon sun, while passing time without counting it. Clock punching did not seem to be one of the town's pastimes. They would need a clock for that anyway.

The fishermen, who reclined near their gossamer wooden boats, had already told us that the only way to continue west would be to drive down the beach. That is, of course, if you can find a way to cross the Miguel de la Borda River, known for its especially deep center depths. So we decided to begin our return journey back to Panama City. Since we were driving around in the area's equivalent of a bus, a ranch hand asked us if he could ride in the back of the pickup. As we toted our new standing passenger, the trio of trendiness approached the truck. Their ringleader aimed a slinky finger at me. "*Tu, llamame*," she soothed.

I shook my head helplessly and responded that I live in the United States. That caused them to rush the window. Mentioning to them that I had a girlfriend back home was also of little use. They still wrote down the numbers of the antenna-towered public phones in the concrete square across from the church.

I did not have the chance to offer an account of Miguel de la Borda's nightlife. But with a town square, a new pier, and time to model boutique apparel, Miguel de la Borda still provided a surprisingly incongruent end to what the roadway approach may have suggested. It was no Beverly Hills, but the town illustrated an inexorable drive to carve out a cheerful living, in spite of address or roofing style.

The best part about returning eastward was that we knew the terrain, since we had just driven through it. The worst part was— well, that we knew the terrain, since we had just driven through it. After we had eased over one of the more challenging passages (a two *patacon* hill, according to Dumas' nibbling metric), I asked Dumas to stop, as I wished for a photo of the troublesome hill. An approaching 4x4 carrying groceries to one of the stores stopped next to me, its driver angling his eyebrows in ruminative attack formation. "What are you doing?"

"I'm taking a picture of the road."

"This is not a road," he spewed. "It's a horse trail! It's garbage! Look at it. Why take a photo of something so ugly?"

It's proof that someone voted for garbage, I wanted to say.

I glanced back at the raw ribbon of mud cut through the voracious jungle that itched to heal the scar across its flesh, as a bulldozer tamed the pathway in the distance in front of us. I attempted to explain to the driver how people who have never driven out to Miguel de la Borda may be interested in knowing what kind of "horse trail" needs to be navigated in order to get there. But it *is* possible—for at least part of the year, that is.

With that answer, he let me return to Dumas' truck and we began to edge our way back east, passing the bulldozer and its newly reshaped road. But where the bulldozer had yet to make its mark, the mud grabbed at the wheels. Eric, Dumas, and I, beginning to pretend we were indifferent to the truck tipping and dipping like a carnival ride, exchanged recipes for *pifá*, a chestnut-like tropical fruit then in season. "I haven't been able to improve upon the traditional recipe of boiling them in salted water for 45 minutes," I contributed amidst a good sideways sloshing.

"For some reason, they taste good with hollandaise sauce," Eric pointed out.

But enough about us. How was our standing room-only passenger in the back? After 20 minutes, we heard a rapping on the roof, or "it's my stop" in Panamanian truck-bed parlance. Commuter delivered. Thank you for riding Costa Abajo Trailways.

* * *

The tropical sun fell in its usual evening haste. We reunited with pavement, which brought us to the queue in front of the swing bridge.

As is the custom, Dumas was cell phoning someone outside his car while waiting for the light to change. Also as is the custom, the light switched to green without warning. Derailed by the excitement, Dumas bobbled his cell phone and began fishing for it in savage desperation under the pickup while the entire queue behind us wrapped around his truck like a hurricane gust. By the time he snared his phone, an eight-wheel truck had already swerved ahead. Due to the swing bridge's weight restrictions, however, the bridge guards held us at the entrance ramp while the truck crept across. Would the light inconveniently turn red for an inconveniently extended time? How late is Restaurante Nani open?

On one axis of the crossing, thousands of tons of hockey gloves, socks, plastic toys, and guitar picks patiently waited in a brutally efficient stack of metal shipping containers on the deck of a cargo vessel. On the other axis sat a lone pickup truck that missed its earlier chance. Which one would the guards choose?

They waved us forward. (Sorry, America, but you are going to have to wait 17 extra seconds to receive your shipment of t-shirts from the factories of Cambodia.)

Dumas extracted us from a realm of more cockfighting rings than paved roads, more beer gardens than strips of developed coastline. We returned to the eastern side of the Canal, en route to Panama City. And with a patacon or two to spare.

4.

Sweetening Life, One Pound at a Time

TRUCKS LADEN WITH STOCKS of freshly harvested cane reeds were buzzing about the Pan-American Highway near the southern city of Aguadulce, leaving a trail of dried leaves scattered on the route. Approaching the end of the dry season, the region was wrapping up its frenzied production of sugar for the year. I met with Santa Rosa refinery's Daniel Quirus for a closer look at the creation of the magnificent spice that Americans happily consume at the rate of 30 kilograms per head annually.

Barely over the hum of whirling machinery, designed to forcefully crush the cane into a sweet juice, Daniel explained how three shifts of factory workers, comprising a fleet of 4000, usher the juice through the machinery, following a particular recipe of boiling, condensing, and crystallizing. The entire process, from open field to sealed bag, takes only 24 hours. The night shift crew earns a little more; all employees, however, can take home some of the fruits of their labor to their kitchens, although after monitoring a dizzying procession of thousands of sugar bags a day, I bet you'd be inclined to lose your sweet tooth. OK, maybe not.

The around-the-clock operation yields 1.5 million pounds of sugar a day, everyday throughout Aguadulce's dry season, which lasts a little over three months. In one scant season, the Santa

Rosa refinery produces enough sugar to make 2.5 billion servings of flan—or one flan with a diameter of 4 kilometers, provided that you have 2 billion eggs on hand.

This output seems surprising when you consider that some of the machines that bag the sugar are 50 years old and still churning proudly, albeit with the occasional burp. As if on cue, one of these veteran machines jammed in front of Daniel and me. But the machine did not stop. Instead, with the dexterity of a professional percussionist, a refinery worker plucked out the recalcitrant paper clog. He timed his grabs perfectly in between the merciless pounding of various metallic arms and hammers. Not a finger was lost.

Unlike many other agricultural industries, the Santa Rosa refinery boasts sustainable agricultural practices. The refinery reuses the same hectares of land to grow cane. Most waste from the process is not waste at all; the plant burns the stalky leftovers from the crushing process to heat its own steam boilers. Used water is cleaned and recycled. Molasses, another by-product of sugar refining, is actually a desirable commodity, utilized by both farmers (to make feed for livestock) and liquor manufacturers (to produce Panama's rum).

While the new cane shoots are diligently photosynthesizing for our benefit during the long rainy season, the refinery effectively shuts down, except for a research project or two. How do the refinery workers find work for the rest of the year? "*Camarones*," Daniel promptly answered. Shrimp. The tasty crustaceans crawling around the cultivation pools of Aguadulce provide income for shrimp farmers, while fortifying local and national restaurants with a bounty ready for the typical preparations of *al ajillo* (garlic sauce), *a la criolla* (sweet tomato and onion sauce), and even on pizza. For landlubbing laborers, the cane fields of nearby Colombia follow a different weather pattern, providing another possibility for seasonal income. Nonetheless, an Aguadulcen cabbie was convinced that many refinery men (no women work in the factory) live a "simple life" during the rainy season while their families take their turn to work.

The refinery not only stocks the kitchens of Panama with its product, it also exports raw sugar to the United States, where it is refined by the latter, avoiding refined sugar's caking issues and import politics alike (refining sugar is one of a shrinking number of industries where the United States is active in protecting its home-turf jobs instead of outsourcing them). America's involvement in the Panamanian sugar industry does not end there, however. Many of the machines used at the refinery have been imported from the United States and are calibrated to the bizarreness of the English system of measurement, which is why the refinery does not sweeten its own country one kilogram at a time — rather one old-fashioned pound at a time. But however one measures it, the flan still tastes delicious.

5.
Secondhand Spirits

AMIDST THEIR CHRISTIAN DEVOTION, many Panamanians, on a daily basis, rely on the assistance bestowed by the *diablo rojo*—the red devil.

Worshiping this nether deity isn't sacrilege. But it isn't exactly painless either. You see, the *diablo rojo* is one of the workhorses of Panamanian public transit—a roaring, exhaust-festooned artifact of the automobile age. The discomfort arises from the *diablo rojo's* close quarters inside, since the fleet was created from refurbished American school buses acquired by mechanically inclined Panamanians at auctions in the States. The seats, designed to accommodate grammar-school femurs, remain firm and defiant.

But the Panamanians have been quite busy isthmus-izing their bargain prizes. Despite being dubbed "red" devils, the buses of Panama City—and beyond—have been fortified indiscriminately from the entire color wheel to portray such subjects as professional wrestling stars, the Panamanian flag, comic strip characters, and even Jesus (as the co-pilot, of course). Every fender, bumper, and wheel succumbs with psychedelic detail. In all of Panama, only the quetzal—a beautiful, intensely colorful creature that shimmers before lucky birders in the western mountains of the country—can outdo the red devil's burst of airbrushed passion.

In a country with such a cavernous income divide, *diablos rojos*, in a perversely audacious way, weave through social fabrics both rich and poor. These roving landmarks growl past the front steps of extravagant Panama City casinos just as often as they deliver illiterate shoppers grasping avocado plants and piglets, up unnamed dirt roads and across the country with tireless regularity. Not everyone rides the bus; I met a few *capitaleños* who admitted to me that they would not know how to navigate bus transfers once they left the city. But, in the end, riders or not, just about everyone standing close to a street or road ends up coughing up the same communal exhaust.

Perhaps out of deference to the quetzal, the ex-school buses roaming the volcano-side town of Boquete (very near the frolicking grounds of the quetzal) are whitewashed. White devils, I suppose. The artists had only been summoned to fashion the obligatory puffy, hand-painted destinations occupying the entire top halves of the windshields. When I needed to depart Boquete for David, a city near the Pacific, I followed the example of the locals and placed my faith in this retrofitted piece of American nostalgia.

Bracing myself against the punishment of the familiar suspension system recalled memories of attempting to finish homework on the grammar school bus, one shaky word at a time. But I doubt I would have completed any assignment had I taken this white devil's journey to school. Along the route, the bus stops and the concrete lean-tos slathered with ongoing political skirmishes would have hopelessly distracted me. Besides the arguments—both sides represented via aerosol—concerning a proposed highway to tear across the pristine north side of the nearby dormant Baru Volcano, I was traveling through Panama in a tense election year, partisan painters hitting every inch of visible concrete. Countless scrawlings of *"Si a la carretera"* (yes to the highway) with its *"Si"* crossed out and replaced with a *"No"* would precede its vice versa on the next bus stop. It was a graffiti connoisseur's pig-out.

Music shooting from pairs of speakers embedded into the bus' walls every 10 feet ensured I was not trundling along in rural New England. Instead of the requisite churns of invigorating merengue and cumbia emanating from most other Panamanian buses and vans, however, my bus driver had been cruising with classic rock. Who would have guessed I'd groove to the guitar licks of the Eagles and Boston when descending from the heights of Central America's spine? After accompanying my upbringing through proms and minimum-wage jobs, "Hotel California" abruptly became music to chip my knees by.

"Cool wind in my hair…" crooned Don Henley, while diesel exhaust, hemorrhaging from an engine that probably hadn't received a tune-up since it left the States on freight ship, freely invaded the bus through the windows and only withdrew when we arrived at David. I pulled my legs out of a peculiar genuflection and paid the driver the fare as he opened the emergency door, then serving as entry to the trunk — that is, the space under the back seats — to fetch my luggage.

My journey had barely begun, since I was headed north for the Atlantic-side island of Bocas Isla. Why, then, did I head south to Pacific-side David? Roads cutting across the continental divide of western Panama are almost as rare as the elusive quetzal. Most of the existing roads drain in parallel like the rivers from the mountains down to David and the Pan-American Highway. This situation simultaneously delights environmentalists but enrages some of the less scrupulous developers, not surprisingly stoking the polarized battle over the newly proposed east-west highway. While the Ngöbe nation, native to the isthmus, has been comfortably and skillfully crossing back and forth over the continental divide via footpaths stomped through the cloud forest for centuries, there is only one vehicular passage that dares to cross the same area of the mountain range. That's where I was headed.

I crawled into a Toyota Coaster, considered either a puffy van or a squashed bus, which plied the soaring route. The vehicle, a tough veteran of an undisclosed number of past lives, wore a crack at one side of its windshield, charmingly *de rigueur* for Panamanian ground transportation. The lightning-shaped fracture featured proudly as if it were some kind of a gang insignia.

As the bus' doorman bungeed my luggage to the roof, I found the only available seat next to a woman donning a traditional billowy Ngöbe dress. Even though she had been shepherding a well-behaved son and a live, bagged chicken, she pushed her cargo into her lap—both livestock and offspring—to make room for me.

Her actions, noble as they were, didn't avail much room, since Coaster seats don't quite span the width of a whole rump (an athletic rump, mind you). Since my seat's foam had decisively given up its perky shape hundreds of cross-isthmus trips ago, I was left with a hollowed-out shell. I was trying to allow more room for the woman and her son by sitting halfway on the seat's aisle-facing ridge, but I kept falling in the cavity. When I finally succeeded in balancing on the edge, I initiated an unintended knee duel with the man across the dinner plate-width aisle.

That was when I discovered that due to such coziness, whatever someone was reading, everyone nearby would be reading as well. Angel, my neighbor across the aisle, had opened a voting instruction guide, one page of which draped into my lap. There was nowhere else for the page to go, so I simply read it along with him. Very informative, actually. Did you know that paper ballots for the Panamanian presidency have photos of the candidates?

After we were both satisfied that we understood the procedure for exercising democracy in Panama, Angel and I mulled over upcoming election politics in both Panama and the States, both of us using Spanish as a second language. I would not have understood Angel's first language, Ngöbere, a native tongue spoken mainly in the Ngöbe's newly formed, semi-autonomous comarca carved out of parts of three Panamanian provinces. His wife, seated next to him, wearing a bright orange Ngöbe dress with triangular bands of trim, remained silent throughout the chat, exercising her political leanings by nodding her crisp new baseball cap with the logo of the presidential candidate they supported toward me. Thanks to repetition of the graffiti crews' work, I easily recognized the cap's colors and insignia. (A month later, the pair's chosen contestant lost in a four-way election to Martín Torrijos, son of an ex-dictator of Panama, under the son's mantra *"cero corrupción,"* or *"*zero corruption," signifying his pledge to distance himself from the country's cherished political tradition.)

As we ascended into the mountains, the air conditioning that fought off the swamp-thick humidity of David became ill fitting for the sudden altitude and was promptly relieved of its duties. The turns became sharper. I kept falling off the seat's ridge. Nervous clucks escaped from the bag in my seatmate's lap. She stabilized her son on her knee while protecting the bag, keeping dinner as fresh as can be. The doorman, normally spending half the ride hanging out the door to collect fares, left his post and utilized the centrifugal forces on the curves to flirt with fashionably dressed young female passengers. I hoped that the doorman had utilized equal effort into securing my luggage to the roof.

The driver paused the tape (that had been treating the Coaster to the rhythm of a steady cumbia) and allowed a few locals peddling bags of green, unroasted coffee beans and peeled oranges for a dollar apiece onto the bus. The passengers were, of course, paying for convenience, since a bag of oranges from an improvised stand in town usually runs about 25 cents.

Somewhere in the high, chilly folds of the divide, I could no longer detect the sight nor smell of slash-and-burn clearing, a farmer's plot-preparing technique otherwise ubiquitous in rural Panama. The unsustainable practice is responsible for destroying an obscene amount of the country's forest—plots only yield marketable crops for a few years until the tropical soil, deprived of nutrients, gives up, then the farmers leave a wasteland behind and move on—yet the practice often provides the sole means of income for poor farmers. Here, however, the unfavorable conditions of the peak elevation have quelled the dilemma.

And then, from far below, emerged the opal awe of the Pacific Ocean and, minutes later, the Atlantic. Had it not been for a few untimely mountains, I might have seen both in one eager, spinning glance. As the majestic green rolls of plunging earth turned me into a wide-eyed kid again (I even caught myself saying "coooool!" a little too loudly), the Panamanians—even the children—remained unphased, finding the cloud forest as familiar as an older sibling.

After the Coaster ducked into a swirl of Atlantic-side turns, the bus slowly began to heat up. We reacquainted ourselves with the powers of the air conditioner, the stinging scent of slash-and-burn plots reappeared on schedule, and the heights of the divide rose farther and farther behind us. The driver decided it was time for lunch.

He parked at an open-aired café at Rambala, a fork in the road for those traveling to the Caribbean coast. As the driver sat down at a picnic-style table for a bowl of *sancocho*, the national dish of chicken soup spiced with *culantro*, the woman sitting next to me whisked away her pre-*sancocho* chicken into another bus departing for the eastern prong of the fork. I bid Angel and his wife farewell while I downed a 25-cent glass of cold, fresh *chicheme*, a sweet corn and milk drink—just what I needed to offset my return to tropical humidity.

The driver waddled back aboard and inserted a merengue tape to get us through the hour of coast-hugging en route to the port of Almirante, my stop. With no more single ladies to pursue, the doorman resumed hanging out of the open door as a sprinkling of thatched-roof pole houses escorted us along.

Near the drop-off intersection, a pair of self-proclaimed guides (local unemployed youths extracting tips as "cab ride facilitators," as I was to discover) ran onto the bus even before it had fully stopped. The doorman climbed onto the roof and retrieved my luggage, which survived the trip over the continental divide unharmed. He proved to be an excellent bungee technician. (I hoped that he had collected a couple ladies' numbers for his other efforts.) The faster of the two guides conducted me into a cab for a short trip to the water taxi port while the other guide, limply observing the transaction, muttered, "I get the next one."

While having my brain shaken like a can of whipped cream on the outboard motorboat taxi to Bocas Isla, the final leg of transit to my destination, I thought how different my journey would have unfolded if I had opted for the quick flight from David to the island. The flight would have reduced a five-hour, climate-capricious trek into a 30-minute hop. It's true that the flight only runs Monday through Friday, and it was Saturday; but even if I had scheduled differently and taken the airplane, there would have been no bags of green coffee beans peddled up the aisle; no stop for a refreshing *chicheme*; and no cumbia. I'd say my faith was rewarded.

6.
Hiking to the Bush Rat Buffet

"IS THERE A HOLE in the boat?" I asked while scooping out water from the hull.

My boatman, covered smugly with a Hawaiian shirt, met my concern with a slow waving of his finger, his other hand working the tiller of the motor. I thought, at first, that a previous rain dumped a minor bounty into the wooden canoe, and a little bailing with the boat's plastic cooking oil jug would take care of it. But 20 minutes into our journey along the coast of Bastimentos Island, I was still chucking water out of the boat, the water level inside remaining insistently steady, like in one of those gag-gift soup bowls.

Fortunately, the water around Bastimentos, like some other swatches of undeveloped Caribbean coast, provides an enchanting turquoise window into the seabed. While my boatman, Balerio, remained hunkered down over the tiller, he exchanged navigation information in the Buglé language with Jorge, my guide, at the front of the boat. Balancing dexterously on hinged feet, Jorge stood at the bow scouring the ripples for discolorations under the surface that might cause trouble.

It was obvious that the duo, both born into the indigenous Buglé communities of the island, had logged many kilometers over water. But so had the boat. Atop its meandering rows of weather-punished lumber planks, rectangles of sheet metal had been tacked inside and outside, in a variety of fascinating angles, forming a veritable headcheese of aquatic transport. I tried not to think about what a tumor of rock-solid coral lying in the shallows would do to the boat.

I was dutifully bailing because I was determined to visit a man who is referred to as a crazy hermit, by some, and a legendary resourceful chef, by others. Polo, a man who named the beach in front of his house after himself, has been living on the northern coast of the island alone for the past 40 years, although I would not call him a hermit. Despite having no connection to the rest of the planet other than a passing boat or a determined hiker, he always seems to attract a few visitors each day, owing to his slow-cooked meals and hospitality, which have been celebrated religiously among backpackers and other dedicated visitors. I was ready to tuck away whatever critter of the day the islander cook would be stewing up.

Since I was staying at a cabana on the southeastern flank of the island, and Polo lived on the north shore, the boat ride should have turned a three-hour, muddy, mountainous hike through a national park into a half-hour boat ride, according to Jorge. Gallons of bails later, however, we arrived as far west as Balerio dared while tempting run-ins with coral. His best seaworthy effort left us on a thin beach about half an hour east of Polo's house before he daintily led the headcheese vessel back out to sea, one hand on the tiller and the other hand flinging jugs of water overboard.

In a lithely percussive squish, Jorge worked his pair of knee-high rubber boots into the mud. I asked him if he knew how to find his fellow islander's abode. "Polo is a good friend of mine," he declared buoyantly. He deemed the terrain on which we were about to tread "easy." The coastal cliffs of the eastern tip, which we had successfully skipped by taking the boat, were apparently not to be reckoned with. He shook his head, losing his square-toothed smile for a moment. "They're like the jungles of Vietnam," he spat.

I was prepared to hike back from Polo's Beach later on, since I didn't want to find myself on the oncoming afternoon waves that the locals had forecasted as seasonally gigantic (I'm sure Balerio would not have been enchanted at the prospect either). But I hadn't prepared for a hike in both directions. I seemed to be a little better prepared, however, than others who had followed the path before me — the mud pools and the slippery slopes served as a graveyard for flip-flops and other footwear inappropriate for a muddy jungle hike. Like notches on a bedpost, the half-submerged collection of flats and tongs sucked off of inattentive feet had speckled the brownness indiscriminately with all colors and styles. They never appeared in pairs. My sneakers, so far, hung on valiantly. Jorge cut through without difficulty, only stopping to empty water out of his boots after we crossed a stream.

"*Espera*" became my favorite word. I often shouted it while pulling my legs out of the mud 20 paces behind Jorge, from whom I should have taken a hint as to the best footwear for the terrain.

During an uncharacteristic pause, Jorge pointed to a bush shooting its spiny leaves outward like a pyrotechnic frozen in mid-burst. "*Piña*," he remarked. Pineapple. But we weren't the only ones to notice. Above us, a clan of white-faced monkeys slinked around in the forest canopy, spreading out and sizing us up. It was, perhaps, this simian inquisitiveness that inspired Christopher Columbus, on his fourth voyage to the Americas, to showcase his conquistador's brand of anthropology, writing that the monkeys of Central America bore faces of men, while the men he encountered were deemed barbarians.

Until recently, the province of Bocas del Toro, in which Bastimentos lies, has not played host to many other outsiders. Slaves from English-speaking colonists of other Caribbean islands trickled into the archipelago in the early 19th century, followed by banana plantations and their armies of workers decades later. Tourism, however, is an especially new arrival. A 1957 guidebook for Americans living in the Canal Zone neglected to mention that a province called Bocas del Toro even existed, and a 1982 edition of the *South American Handbook*, when mentioning the province, offered the comment "no tourist ever goes there." A new highway connected the mainland portion of the province to the rest of the country only five years before my arrival.

Roads, however, have not reached the island of Bastimentos. Walking paths, instead, serve as the island's arteries, like the one Jorge and I followed with insectile diligence. Along some stretches, the path ran down to the beach, denying us the shade from old-growth jungle. "*Espera*," I announced from behind but, fortunately, trees laden with sea grapes slowed him down. These marble-sized juice bombs resemble their cousins that are crushed for wine in more temperate zones. The main distinction is that shiny, lily pad-shaped leaves underneath each bunch of sea grapes bestow them with the likeness of either props for a B-movie or a poisonous mistake. Fortunately, they were neither. Jorge pillaged one of the trees of its reddest, ripest treats and tossed them into his mouth. After I caught up and tried a few, I figured out how to gnaw around the outside of the grapes, sucking all the tart-sweet juice out while spitting out the bitter core.

The nectar proved a timely appetizer. We approached a small clearing in the path ahead, revealing a branch hung horizontally between coconut palms. We found the work of Polo's uncomplicated landscaping.

* * *

The hike was not my first time setting off to visit Polo. It was my first time hiking to his beach, however. Five months before, I left for his beach by boat from Bocas Isla, the most developed island of the archipelago and a few miles from Bastimentos. I was staying at a hotel in Bocas Town, the largest town of the island, where seared shoulders of spring breakers bobbed up and down the strip of restaurants and boating offices, and boatmen unceremoniously chucked empty beer cans into the bay before docking. Afternoons swam in a mischievously viscous heat, the kind of heat that might embalm you if you forgot to move for some time, like being in a tar pit.

But the ultraviolet index failed to preempt hunger. Despite the concentration of eateries, however, I could not escape rubbery, uninspired shellfish passed off at several of Bocas Town's waterfront restaurants as "island cuisine." After three such meals at three different establishments, and a fourth whose special house sauce atop its octopus turned out to be watered down ketchup, I decided to turn to the tales I had heard of a man named Polo on an island a few miles to the east and began to locate a boatman who knew the way. The boating offices on Bocas Isla were eager to provide a boat to the peaceful waters around the prolific snorkeling meccas in between the islands and the mainland, but they told me that the surf that day was too dangerous for a motorboat to travel to Polo's house. I'd need the boatman to drop me off on the southwestern side of Bastimentos, necessitating an hour walk somewhere to the northern side. And back. I had agreed.

I asked Gabriel, my boatman, where he would drop me off and pick me up. Gabriel, a native of the archipelago, squinted at the horizon and then turned to me. "It would be faster if we go all the way to Polo's Beach," he answered. According to the boating office, wasn't that dangerous?

"Not for me," Gabriel shot back, tapping his chest solidly.

Was his confidence a chimera of sun-crazed machismo or a culmination of 20 years of experience in the waters of the archipelago? I let my stomach make the call. We were going into the open Caribbean to see what Polo was cooking.

As we rounded the northwestern tip of Bastimentos Island, the late dry-season winds sent the sea into a livid pulsation. We couldn't hug the coast owing to coral lurking just under the water surface, so he motored farther out. Before I realized it, we had ridden far into swells as tall as me, their ravines like endless rows of jaws. To avoid capsizing, Gabriel took them head on.

The tiny fiberglass hull slammed down in between waves in an abusive rhythm of belly flops. As I tried to decide whether or not getting eaten by a shark was a noble way to die, I peeked back at Gabriel, who was standing up with feet spread, one hand on to the tiller and the other slightly out for balance like a surfer. But he would not be indulging any penchant for tube riding. He was standing up to get a better view of the army of waves approaching and to plan accordingly, each swell at a time. The steadiness of the belly-flop tempo began rendering a certain comfort, since the steadiness demonstrated that Gabriel was in control of the boat.

That tempo gently faded out when Gabriel turned into the coast to navigate us in between lumps of coral. The water near the beach suddenly flattened out, as if it had tired itself out in anger. Gabriel landed directly in front of the path to Polo's home.

A few steps into a small clearing, we encountered a lean, half-naked figure bent up under the weathered planks of a pole house. He sat motionless, fixating on the smoke and sizzle radiating from a wood fire.

Our approach had activated the man wrenching himself out from under the spindly structure, his face falling into a comfortable grin. He extended a coarse mitt of a hand. "I'm Polo. Da roughest man on da beach."

"I've heard you're a great cook," I said.

"Eh, I don' know nuttin bout cookin," Polo replied, while a pot behind him burbled with excitement.

I attempted a different angle. "What's for lunch?"

Only Polo knew, since his plot facing the Caribbean Sea does not have a phone line. Or a fax machine. Or a web page. Or electricity. Or running water. His only potable water arrives when either someone brings in bottles from Bocas Isla via boat or he catches it during a rainstorm (I had arrived in March, the end of the four-month dry season).

Nor is there a set dining hour—difficult to arrange when he doesn't have a clock anyway. To find out what's for lunch, you just show up.

He waved me over to his fire pit, a pile of glowing wood in a raised hole of earth. Something was stewing noisily in an aluminum pot—the same kind of cookware I'd found at discount department stores in Panama City for $5. Its bottom, scorched black, was balanced atop a few rusted girder scraps. He pulled off a piece of sheet metal that served as the pot's lid, revealing a tumbling stew with a woodsy, meaty aroma.

"Try this," Polo commanded, as he hunched over the pot with a large spoon and gently pushed the gruel my way. But gruel it was not. I was surprised by its spicy richness.

"Not done yet," Polo remarked. "Gotta wait a couple hours. Chicken stew an' rice."

"It looks like you know how to cook."

"Here, lemme show ya somethin'." He turned around, still hunched, and pointed to a row of bottled spices on the floor of his house—marmalade, *salsa de barbacoa*, peanut butter, packets of consommé, and a two-liter bottle that had been refilled with a brown sludge. He grabbed the last item labeled simply POLO in handwritten letters over a piece of masking tape. "A German friend a' mine from Costa Rica made me this. Curry sauce."

He waddled back over to the pot, lifted up the sheet metal, and shook in a few globules of the German-Costa Rican concoction. "Not too much of this," he said as he pointed at me, "or it'll fuck it up!"

He reunited with his lit cigarette, shaking most—and maybe even all—said condiments into the pot, along with whatever ash happened to fall in.

By then, a gaggle of characters just "showed up." A surfer still in his wet suit, lamenting how the winds were interfering with his sport, opened a bottle of beer on a nail protruding from the house's wall. A few dread-locked islanders appeared, having walked from the Afro-Panamanian community on the western edge of the island. Another boat had braved the surf and just moored off the beach, bringing in a lobster-backed couple hungry for the daily offering. A backpacker had begun to negotiate a price to stay at Polo's beach for a few days.

"You want to stay here, $10 a night," Polo answered as he tossed a few chunks of something—fish, I suspected—into the stew pot. "You get a hammock. You can eat three meals a day. Five if you want. Same price."

Using coconut juice for the cooking liquid, Polo doused the rice and lentils. "I have thousands of coconuts," he rumbled as he waved his hand around. "Dem fall in piles." To finish the preparation, he placed a few shiny, heart-shaped leaves on top of the steaming rice pot. "Sea grips," he told me, pointing to the leaves. "Yuh don' know sea grips? Yuh travel all over and yuh don' know nuttin bout sea grips? Fuck!" I must confess, I had never heard of a sea grip before. But I learned quickly that it imparted a sensually fruity flavor into the rice.

What exactly was a sea grip anyway? I began to swirl up images of a thick, demented mangrove that dug its roots into stony coral, gripping on like an alligator's bite to combat the current, ensnarling any vessel ignorant enough to cross its nest of appendages. How did Polo manage to cut off a few of its glossy leaves and return without ending up as vulture food?

How indeed. A little botanical comparison along the beach revealed later—far too late, in fact, to redeem myself—that his Caribbean pronunciation had been referring to another use of the docile sea *grape* tree.

His other verbal nuances proved more festive. As lunch was simmering, Polo continued to use the word "fuck" in the same way most everyone else uses a period to end a sentence. For example: "Go to Bocas. Get my ice—fuck!" Or: "All you can eat, same price—fuck!" Or the most common usage, which makes for inventive parsing: "Fuck—fuck!"

Perhaps I had met with difficulty understanding Polo because, according to a clan of linguists, the Afro-Panamanian community on Bastimentos speaks their own distinct variety of Creole English that developed in isolation on the island over the past century. Linguists who call themselves "creolists" have teased out enough bound morphemes and preverbal periphrastics from the islanders' everyday speech to devote a slew of dry academic journal articles to a subtle variety spoken by only about 600 people. The efforts work out to about 30 words per islander. The sum may seem trifling, but if attention were given to the American variety of English in the same proportion of words-per-speaker, the study would fill 9,000 encyclopedia-sized volumes, counting about 127 volumes dedicated exclusively to the usage and proliferation of the contraction "y'all."

Soon the hour arrived when Polo called upon his congregation to pounce upon the stew and rice. "I got britt-fruit too. Yuh know britt-fruit? You come back and eat five plates if your belly can hold it. Same price!" (More on britt-fruit later.)

The stew pot transformed seemingly mundane ingredients — chicken parts, fish chunks, and sauces from a bottle — into a tingly-soft treat. How did he do it? The smoke from the wood fire sneaking into the stew can undoubtedly claim some credit, as can his friend's bottle of untold murkiness.

But the most likely ringleader of flavor was time. Time spent underneath Polo's house while he enlightened his guests with unbridled lore of brothels on the other side of the island, stocking "1,000 pussies." (The population of the island barely tops 1,000.) Time spent wondering where he obtained the fresh water for the stew.

Even a good meal can't satisfy everyone, however. The backpacker continued to argue that Polo had raised his hammock rate, according to a friend of the backpacker's. "It was always $10," Polo blasted. "Your friend, him tellin' lotta lies — fuck! I'm Polo. Da roughest man on da beach!" He began pounding his chest, bare except for a few curly strands of silver hair. There were no more attempts at haggling for a hammock.

* * *

Jorge and I found "The Roughest Man on the Beach" sleeping on the sand, curled up like a puppy. He was clothed in nothing more than what looked like his only pair of shorts. With a robust bark Jorge called to him. A head began to unwind from the flesh pile; eyelids would open on their own schedule.

I was beginning to realize that taking his time was one of Polo's virtues. Five months ago, I had noticed that a bench fashioned from wood scraps at the entrance to his clearing bore the letters POL carved on its back, presumably the start of an etching that would read POLO'S BEACH. After five months, the carving remained comfortably stalled at the same three letters.

Polo was still reclined on the sand, glancing up at Jorge and me. "What's for lunch?" I asked.

The glowing man pushed himself off the sand and led us under the selection of oblong skulls dangling from the palms at the entrance. Sprawled on the tree-branch smoking rack above the pit, an assemblage of tiny, four-legged carcasses were slowly barbecuing. "Bush rat," Polo answered, scratching his back. "Yuh got any smokes?"

It had been a slow day at Polo's Beach. The afternoon waves, predicted to be rough, hadn't rippled in yet but, nonetheless, successfully scared off boat traffic from arriving. No one that morning had brought in a boatload of beer, soda, ice, and cigarettes—just about the only items Polo needs from town. Even Gabriel hadn't stopped by. Only a couple bottles of beer and soda, left over from several days ago, remained in the cooler. Reclined underneath the pole house, a duo of islanders, the only other visitors, had earned their stay the night before, since they were the ones who hunted the bush rat for today's fixin's.

"Yuh gotta spear 'em," Polo said. Like people, the bush rats have a taste for breadfruit, which is why hunters on the island use pieces of the treat to attract the 5-pound rodents. Despite their sharp claws and fierce, stained teeth, the agoutis—or bush rats, to borrow the Afro-Antillean nomenclature—are avid vegetarians. They are far from the rodents feared as vicious, sore-ridden beasts that chew their way through solid plaster walls to gain access to your potato chips, eat unattended children, and tear apart the alligators in the New York City subway system. Instead, the timid agoutis of Central America use their choppers, in anticlimactic fashion, to gnaw open nuts and tropical fruits that have fallen to the ground. Their claws dig burrows where they normally hide out in the daytime.

The hunters start the search at night when the agoutis emerge from their burrows and forage in the foliage spanning almost the entire interior of the island. Only the agoutis inside the park boundaries are off limits. But the islanders are fortunate that most of the jungle on the island remains intact. According to the people I had met from a Buglé village on the other end of the island, the jungle cultivates an agouti population large enough to presently support hunting — in painful contrast to many areas on the mainland that have been stripped of trees for agricultural and livestock interests.

"Dem rat fast," Polo said, employing a series of scurrying finger motions. "If yuh miss, yuh get nuttin but dirt an' da rat runs off wid jah britt-fruit."

I glanced over at the victorious hunters, who were still resting up from their night of hurling spears. Their pink eyes as thin as cracked pistachios, they both acknowledged my gratitude with big, slow nods floating about in the air, nods that never quite came down again.

Polo indulged my curiosity as I examined the preparations for lunch. "Gotta soften 'em up first," he remarked, referring to the catch on the smoking rack. Polo had used all the German-Costa Rican curry sauce, so he doubled up on his other bottled condiment offerings while I snorkeled around the rainbow of fish hanging around the coral in front of his beach.

The only other visitors of the day, a couple of Panamanian policemen, hiked to Polo's house along the beach from the west just in time for the feast. "C'mon, grab yuh plate, yuh know what to do," Polo announced. Following his orders, I fetched a plate from the raft table and helped myself to the pots of meat and fried plantains, buffet style.

My hike had been compensated well. His bush rat entwined the maddening satisfaction of pork, the miniature joints of rabbit, and the kiss of slow cooking. "Life's too short to eat bad food, agreed?" the islander asked.

Polo emerged from a brief trip into his backyard—the open jungle—with an avocado and sliced it open. Picking avocados hasn't always been a prerogative, at least in the eyes of a small cabal of real-estate investors who, a few years ago, viewed him as a nuisance to their plans to carve up portions of the island that are outside the national park. Polo decided to exercise his squatter's rights, since he had been spearing bush rats on the very same isolated piece of earth decades before investors began realizing how marketable waterfront land in Panama has become. Even the former mayor of Bocas Town tried his hand at evicting squatters and selling the land to investors, only to score a jail cell instead.

After obtaining legal counsel, Polo won his case as well. His success could serve as an example for others. But I was simply curious as to how he did it. "It's over," Polo answered squarely, swatting the air. "No white people gonna get Polo's beach!"

Up until this point, the afternoon had remained blissfully free from the concerns of time. But since Jorge and I needed three hours for the return hike, we had to leave at once. It being half past three, we had to reach the cabanas before the equatorial sun set abruptly at around seven. No one—not even the proudest islander—recommended a hike in the forest at night.

I checked my water stocks. I was running low—only about 6 ounces, not enough for a three-hour hike, half of which would follow the national park's wide beach, all the while our flesh providing fodder for the keenly voracious sun. I had drunk way too much water on the short hike to lunch, a dilemma I deemed fixable by buying a bottle from Polo. But alas, no boats arrived today, thus no restocking of provisions. He gave us a little rainwater that he had collected a day ago, seeming to disregard his own water needs. I suspect Polo subsides on beer alone.

On the hike eastward, I sucked the precious juice out of a few handfuls of sea grapes until we entered the park at the western end of the 6-kilometer Long Beach. But we were not to encounter a well-maintained booth lined with postcards and plastic key chains. Not even a few bored government employees. Instead, the jungle ahead of us was the same jungle behind us, without a marked border of any kind. I took Jorge's word for it that we were in a park. Only a sprinkling of broken flip flops enshrined in the path indicated any kind of previous human presence.

Our sweaty ectoplasm conducted us across the beach, leading us to the entry of the path into the jungle that burrows towards the south side of the island. My tongue had become a hung-over iguana, scales and all. The trail of footwear had ominously stopped. I lost the sound of Jorge's boots farting out a steady march through the mud over the hill in front of me. I stumbled up the mire of rain forest mountains while considering just how I could have failed to realize the seriousness of not bringing enough water, my heart punching out a hardcore B-side, my scales attempting to form the word *espera* several times, to which Jorge yelled back that *agua fresca* waited for us ahead—*fresquita* was his exact word.

Atop the next slope, he dunked his head in an arm-width stream that tumbled so innocently near its headwaters that it had not yet had a chance to be choked with the usual enrichments of farm runoff, garbage, and sewage. I, too, splashed the coolness over my body and drank what seemed like half the creek. Each velvety mineral of the water stroked my entire palate like a well-balanced *Côte-Rôtie*. We might have been lapping up a spring of extraordinary mineral makeup—the kind that hastens the pulse of bottled water devotees—but, most likely, my sun-baked thirst, as sun-baked thirst is wont to do, decided to exploit the flavor of regular water and remodeled it into some acutely thrilling religious experience.

Adorable poison-dart frogs dotted the rest of the forested journey. Football-shaped cacao pods growing off the side of the trunks protruded into the path. Wild gatherings of banana trees saturated the air with a scent so sweet, it's no wonder why so many tropical cultures steam rice and other foods wrapped in their leaves. A sloth, clamped onto a naked branch above us, couldn't give a rat's ass either way.

Let us not forget the bananas themselves. We soon happened upon neatly arranged rows of a few dozen-banana trees—a small *finca* under the forest canopy. The Buglé villages must not be far away.

In lieu of any markings that delineated national park from private land, fresh lumps of cow dung supplied a hint. A few sips of water later, the outlines of thatch-roof houses of a Buglé village clearing broke through the thinning jungle. Jorge slid through a barbed wire fence as if he were taunting me with a magic trick. No matter how gingerly I bent the wires around my limbs, I became ensnared. Jorge diplomatically hid his thoughts behind a smile. I had logged almost three hours across virtually untamed nature, only to spill blood upon a piece of human civilization.

The welcoming committee of Bryan Creek, a half dozen cows and a bull chewing grass, gazed curiously at the mud-pasted humans marching through their pasture. Jorge trudged up the village's hill to a pole house the size of a van, a dozen children peeking out from every gap in its walls. A tidy array of goats, chickens, and dogs hung around under the house while a few more chickens possessed the privilege of roaming inside the house itself.

Jorge had approached the ark to procure a boatman to take us back to the cabanas, since a quick trip down the river at Bryan Creek would save us an hour more of hiking. Our odds improved when none other than Balerio, still modeling his clean, colorful Hawaiian shirt, appeared from one of the half-dozen houses.

Could he motor us back? Yes. But I was short of cash. I probed my backpack for anything I could trade, finding a CD from my now-retired rock band. I clumsily pitched the offer before I had realized that the village didn't have electricity. What use would he have for a music CD?

Balerio's eyes widened. "You mean you want to trade the CD in exchange for a boat ride?"

I was unsure whether he was rather insulted or rather interested, so I revealed why I deemed the disc precious by pointing to the picture on the backside of the jewel case. "That's me. The music is rock," I pleaded. "If you can't play it, you can always sell it—"

"I can play CD's," Balerio responded, clutching the CD close to him. Of course he can play it. I had underestimated the resourcefulness of the Buglé communities of the island, and such a short memory I had flaunted, because the day before, I had visited another of the inland villages where bare feet marched through mud more efficiently than shoes, and the baseball that the kids tossed around was made of a tight ball of tape. Batteries and radios have easily fit aboard dugout canoes en route to Brian Creek. The deal was closed.

Sadly, someone had taken the headcheese vessel out for a bail-intensive ride, leaving us another plank boat—well weathered but insipidly watertight—the only other boat under the droopy thatch roof that serves as Bryan Creek's port. Even if the boat had required a feverish scooping to keep it from sinking, we didn't ride it long enough for such excitement to transpire. After a few minutes' worth of snaking down to the coast, Balerio had quickly earned his taste of New York City pop-punk thrills.

As he prepared to motor away from the cabana's dock, I noticed a harmonica protruding from his back pocket. "I'm a musician," Balerio tendered with undisguised pride. I had found the right person for the trade.

I believe I have now optimized the visitor's checklist of fortifications for a successful, slow-cooked lunch on Bastimentos Island: plenty of bottled water, rubber boots, cigs for the cook, and a modest supply of round, plastic, laser-readable boat fares.

7.

A Toast to Mother Earth

AN INDIGENOUS NATION does not often gain autonomy through a successful uprising against colonial oppression. On February 25th, 2005, Kuna Yala, a province of Northeastern Panama, celebrated the 80th anniversary of the Kuna Revolution by reenacting the events that re-established Amerindian control over the community's traditional coastal territory, including a strip of mountainous, game-hopping tropical forest and over 300 islands.

Trappings of such power greeted Melanie and me when we arrived at the dock of Isla Tigre, one of the islands in the archipelago, to witness the octogenarian celebration. A hand-painted sign facing the dock announced the province's own laws for conduct for visitors and international trade vessels. A kiosk collected Kuna-imposed tariffs. Panamanian policeman were nonexistent.

The political topography curved much differently a century ago, however. Panama had been granting concessions to companies itching to carve up natural resources in Kuna Yala (which translates roughly to "Land of the Kuna"), a gossamer curl of land on the isthmus' northeastern coast that the government viewed as an integral piece of her territory and, thus, could be exploited just like any other non-titled expanse. Outsiders began to extract coconuts, vegetable ivory (nuts from a tagua palm tree), lumber from her jungles, and turtle meat from her waters. The government encouraged cash-crop farmers to settle on Kuna land, since the government viewed the Kuna's sustenance culture as a waste of a natural resource.

The Kuna, as you can imagine, did not share the government's vision. The Kuna, an Amerindian nation that has lived in the region since before the arrival of a certain Genoan explorer, believed they were protecting the land of their deity Mother Earth. Such beliefs attracted the zealousness of missionaries, to whom the government of Panama blissfully gave the nod, for the ruling conservatives in Panama City viewed missionaries as the first step in civilizing a "savage" race.

But perhaps the Kuna's previous interactions with Western trading vessels and passing pirates had numbed the novelty and mystique of Christianity. Many Kuna were converted, but a good number simply acted out convincing genuflections and enjoyed their free Spanish and English schooling.

Meanwhile, Panamanian police moved onto the islands, building dance halls to encourage a breakdown in the Kuna's tradition of arranged weddings. The police fined women wearing nose rings and traditional leg-bindings and banned consumption of *inna*—the Kuna's customary tipple fermented from corn and sugar—along with the day-long slosh-fests, sometimes longer, associated with its enjoyment.   To enforce rules of Western civility, a conservative Jesuit priest introduced stocks. (There's nothing quite like demonstrating how highly refined one's culture is by embracing the use of a medieval punishment device.)

The police began beating islanders who would not comply with the pacification. Soon any activity viewed as uncivilized, such as picking lice out of a family member's scalp—a common task necessitated by the communities living in such close quarters—became grounds for a bludgeoning.

But things were about to get uglier. In February of 1925, on several islands partaking in the Panamanian festival of *carnival*, an import of the occupation, the Kuna carefully orchestrated the ambush of the resident policemen. On Isla Tigre, one of the most gruesome theaters of the revolution—and where we had just arrived—beckoning islanders lured the community's two policemen into the dance hall, promptly beat one to death, and felled the other with an axe. Not completely satisfied, the villagers brought the latter's corpse to a remote island and chopped it up into small pieces to assist the vultures. (One might acquire the impression that the Kuna just want to be left alone.)

The revolution's work did not end with the massacre of almost a dozen colonial policemen. On other islands, some of the most rabid, axe-swinging rebels finally crossed off the last few entries on their executioners' checklists by dispensing with indigenous policemen viewed as traitors. The remaining police fled for their lives and never returned, their absence leaving the region with an uncertain status, incrementally gaining acceptance until 1953, when Panama City officially recognized the region as an autonomous province with its own government and a defined border. Kuna Yala still encounters scattered invasions by farmers and loggers along their unmonitored border, but the comarca now possesses the legal right to expel them. Chalk one up for Mother Earth.

When we climbed up from the dock, I wondered how the island would be reenacting their revolution. But the islanders that greeted us told us that the reenactment had already ended. We knew we were late, however. With help from a renegade trade wind, a plane from one of Panama's local airlines had crashed on another of the notoriously short and tricky runways of Kuna Yala a few weeks before, whittling the already quaint supply of airplanes down to a dysfunctional pulp. On the morning of our flight, the remaining aircraft had been buzzing feverishly from the capital to the islands and back in an attempt to cover all the routes and brought us to nearby Narganá four hours late.

But it wasn't too late to party. For the past 11 days, the community of Isla Tigre had been preparing copious quantities of *inna* — known as *chicha fuerte* in Spanish — buried in underground urns. At the dock, the soccer-ball eyes and mask-like grin of islander Deobaldo escorted us around the island, his *inna* breath playfully orbiting him like a loyal dog. Only the size of a few football fields, the island shoehorned its cane walled and concrete dwellings closely along its maze of packed dirt walkways. I failed to find the dance hall left over from the island's colonial interlude; I would imagine the islanders had destroyed it quite some time ago. Deobaldo invited us to the fast-arriving wet portion of the celebration (notwithstanding his unofficial sampling at an undisclosed point earlier in the day).

Anticipation of an alcoholic libation, especially one unknown to me, called for a base coat of something solid. While the revolt prevented Panama from exporting politics to the province, the Kuna have not hesitated from bringing in *a la carte* elements from the rest of the country when it suits them, as was the case of a Panamanian-style café/grocery store serving meals for cash near the dock. At the café, the Refresqueria y Fonda Digir, Melanie and I, along with our boatman, put back plates of the Refresqueria's only lunchtime offering — rice fried with onions, eggs, and chunks of Panama's quotidian canned meat matter.

Our boatman, Pepito, a 59-year-old native of the islands, taught us the Kuna words for every edible sea creature in the surrounding seas. His stone blue eyes cut through a sun-tortured Amerindian face, speaking almost as much of a particular, once-taboo coupling during generations past (Kuna custom used to forbid marriages of Kuna to outsiders) as his outdoor profession.

Basketball trophies stood over bins selling knobby pieces of *ñame*, a gastronomic workhorse of a tuber found in kitchens across the isthmus. Today, however, they simply served as a doorstop. As the radio picked up a Journey song from a mainland rock radio station, the cooks and waitresses, girls donning dresses spiked with panels of molas — colorful, hand-embroidered works that have become a Kuna cultural watermark — pushed their long hair away from cheeks brightened red with *achiote*. Their silky black locks still intact, the staff had not reached puberty, for in Kuna society, at least on the more traditional islands like Isla Tigre, when a girl enters her first menstrual cycle, her hair is cut short — a custom once banned by the colonial authorities.

Unlike the cane reed walls of most of the island's houses, the Refresqueria's concrete walls provided a nice flat surface for bright, hand-painted images of seafood and decorative flourishes adapted from mola designs. Some flirtations with Western culture flaunt themselves overtly, ranging from the emergence of zinc roofing instead of thatch and the construction of well-manicured fields for soccer and volleyball. But another borrowing has turned up in a more solemn niche: the island denies attendance of important events like today's to any man not wearing long trousers. As I was to discover, only length — not style — mattered. I had achieved the required level of decorum by donning a pair of old sweatpants borrowed from my guesthouse's owner on Narganá Island, who had tipped me off to such a practice.

When I had first seen the island from the boat, I had imagined the bare-calf ban tenuous at best, since a forest of spiny masts from visiting sailboats had encircled the island. How could the island keep all that Bermuda-shorts cash at bay? But once the urns were tapped, I only noticed one more pair of Western men sitting inside the long community house, the place where *inna* would be drunk, and their calves remained sheathed as well.

A felt hat silhouette in the center of the long house started into a somber singsong chant. Men had filled up the benches on one side of the dark building, women on the other. I was ushered in to sit near the head *saila*, or chief, who was surveying the procession through patiently fixed eyes, half-slit, and seeming to merely supplement a keener sense of some kind. He sat in the complete fashion ensemble for the formal Kuna man, including a felt hat embroidered with a mola design, an untucked dress shirt drawn in at the neck with a theatrically wide red tie, and bare feet poking out from his slacks.

Deobaldo's grin grew elastic as he bobbed atop rubber legs. In one of his hands, a wrap of tobacco the size of a dynamite stick trailed his movements with sweet swirls of smoke. He approached a row of elders and, still dancing, blew a gust of smoke under their hats. As the Kuna use tobacco smoke for purposes of healing (don't tell your pulmonologist), the recipients froze in satisfied gazes. Deobaldo bounced over to the second highest *saila* and treated his face to a generous dose of the secondhand vapors, the *saila* indulgingly leaning into the haze as if he were receiving a massage.

The men were to drink first and formed a line. The blackened faces and hands of a girl painted in jagua, ink formed by boiling the fruit of a tropical tree, greeted each man in the serving line with a small half gourd filled with plain water. The man then swished out his mouth to cleanse it and, in a decisive lunge, spit onto the packed dirt floor, the same earth that has faithfully soaked up untold years of party-time backwash. Another jagua-blackened girl filled up a tiny vessel with the *inna* and poured it into the man's half gourd, four times, to create one serving.

The revelers encouraged me to try. I figured a *mergi*—the Kuna word for a person from The States—shouldn't disappoint his hosts, so I did my best to mimic those before me. Trying not to feel self-conscious about an activity that might otherwise appear uncouth, I launched the gourd's water onto the floor in a clean shot—well, as clean as spitting gets. My hosts approved, for small inked hands then passed me a larger gourd, its sloshing depths opaquely black.

How can I describe the libation? Without a point of reference, the task may prove difficult but, technically, the fermented liquid is a type of wine. Its entry in one of the enological industry rags might sound something like "Ringing in the 80th anniversary, the 2005 Kuna Revolution *inna* reveals a nose profile of toasted corn, pond scum, and charcoal. The jet-black color of this offering hints at its unctuously thick body and powerful finish of used motor oil and Irish stout. Accompany with tobacco and canned meat. Drink now."

Women had formed an *inna* line as smoke and chatter twirled together under the roof of the long house. "*Momo* is a good word to know," a reveler announced from atop his limber frame, leaning into me. "In Kuna, it means 'drunk.'" His head swung in front of mine like a balloon, an expectant stare. His unsolicited translation services continued with words for favored parts of the female, starting with the colloquial expression for the reproductive organ. I didn't quite catch its translation, the multisyllabic term proving quite a—well—mouthful.

After another round of gourd pours, the party began bouncing out onto the streets, a train of pipe flute players dancing under a minor key melody while shaker gourds mapped out the steps, until the jam fell apart in laughter. After another round, the tropical sun reaching optimum scorch, several women in full dress, from leg binding to colorful headscarves, began to light cigarettes in their mouths by doing push-ups on top of other lit cigarettes carefully stuck into the dirt of the pathways.

After another round, one reveler felt it necessary to mention that he was not wearing any underwear.

It was only early afternoon and, since the *inna* had achieved such unhindered results in so little time, I wondered if, as a guest, I was expected to stick around until the vat was empty. Indeed, I found it ambitious to gauge the proper etiquette in a place where you are encouraged to blow smoke in the elders' faces and spit on the floor. As I began feeling the true meaning of the word *momo*, cockeyed thatch roofs and all, we decided we should leave before another gourd was summoned.

*   *   *

If I take away only one lesson after visiting Kuna Yala, it would be to refrain from interpolating the customs of all islands based on one. At times, it seemed that the only common thread across the communities was the comarca's unwavering sense of independence, perhaps itself responsible for spawning healthy variety within the Kuna nation. While drinking alcohol is outlawed in some communities, save traditional events, the activity flourishes on others. Allegiances to religions and political parties change from island to island (and from family to family). Some communities allow outsiders to stay the night, while others forbid it, as they have since first interacting with Westerners.

But I encountered the most naked contrast when traveling between Isla Tigre and Narganá, an island just half an hour to the east. Narganá, where I had arranged for lodging at a concrete guesthouse, had brewed no *inna*, for it did not celebrate the anniversary cherished by the more traditional islands, nor did any axe meet with a policeman's spine here 80 years ago. Ironically, many of the practices the Kuna had fought for are scarcely exercised on Narganá, owing to the island's peculiar history of regular exposure to Western imports. The most ostentatious example, women choosing t-shirts, jeans, and skirts over beaded leg bindings and mola-emblazoned dresses, has rendered the island of little value to package tour itineraries promising its clients a cursory chance to gawk at an "exotic" culture "unchanged" for hundreds of years.

Nonetheless, Narganá is still a dynamic mixture of its Kuna heritage and whatever ideas have been brought in from the docks. Cane-walled houses sprout satellite television dishes from their thatched roofs. Just a short walk from the province's only bank, a thicket of over-the-water outhouses constructed from mismatched pieces of rusty zinc radiate from the coast. Patrolling through the dirt streets straightened long ago during the Panamanian occupation, fishermen swagger under buckets of their day's catches, alternately shouting "*Pe'cado*" and "*Ua*," the respective Spanish and Kuna words for the commodity. On some of the more conservative Kuna islands further east like Ukupseni, no outsiders are permitted to live on the island, and any Kuna who marries an outsider must leave the community. Paco, the *mestizo* Panamanian owner of the guesthouse, lives on Narganá in his cinder-block house with his Kuna wife.

In the center of the island, I encountered a more permanent symbol of the community's direction: a town square with a statue. A centerpiece of the island, the admittedly Western homage of a bronze figure was not unsuitable for a European roundabout. The figure portrayed the squat frame of Charly Robinson, one of the first literate Kuna who was instrumental in encouraging education. He was the man the government of Panama thought was going to assist in pacifying the Kuna from the inside, but instead, the fruits of educating the Kuna ended up provisioning the logistics for the revolution.

The name of the island connected to Narganá via a footbridge, Corazon de Jesus (the heart of Jesus)—if you hadn't guessed already—speaks of its preferred countenance. The village may have appeared as any average rural Panamanian town, had it not been for the over-the-water pigpens and outhouses extending from the edges of the island. The brutally effective sound systems of the island's clubs introduced the island to me when I was still standing on the Narganá side across the channel. When I approached the island's ground zero of nightlife, churning dancehall beats bulged into its plaza, which revolved around a statue of—appropriately—Jesus. If aliens landed at the square of Corazon de Jesus (instead of the usual supposed places in Missouri with names like Old Pebble and Turdville), the visitors might gather that the statue in the center of the plaza represented the god of partying.

As progressive as the duo of islands has become, however, Corazon de Jesus still lacks potable water, even though its neighbor Narganá has succeeded in conquering geography by running a pipe down from the mainland mountains. On Corazon de Jesus, I met a young woman from the Peace Corps who, when not hugged and teased by throngs of giggly girls from the island, was assisting in locating a solution to the tricky engineering issue of either extending the pipes from Narganá (ensuring that there is enough water pressure for both islands) or running a new set of pipes to the mountain source. No matter: attaining the decibels of an East Village dance club, the island pounded out its nightly revelry without running water and without *inna*. But I would bet the cases of iced beer helped.

* * *

Conservative or progressive, thatch roof or zinc, molas or halter-tops—the barriers of nature affect all Kuna island communities indiscriminately. Perhaps the most illustrative of these difficulties arrived gradually, but surely, over the past 30 years. It involves the spiny lobster, a spotted crustacean particular to the reefs of the Caribbean Sea and a part of the Kuna diet (and a tasty addition to the diets of Kuna Yala's visitors).

I was far from the first to find the spiny lobster sweeter than its counterpart from the cool waters off New England. And that was the problem. What used to amount to a few lobsters ending up in the galleys of passing sailboats developed into daily prop-plane shipments out of the region, once the Kuna began constructing runways to connect their virtually road-free comarca to the rest of the country in the 1970s. The more the *langostero*, or lobsterman, could catch, the more dollars he could secure for a motor for his dugout canoe, gasoline, rum, or anything else he could not grow or make himself.

By the 1990s, the ecological consequence was clear — the lobster population had paid for the divers' profits. The divers needed to dive much deeper to find the succulent crustaceans, only to bring up fewer. When I asked Pepito, he recalled that the lobstermen used to catch more than 20 lobsters a day, apiece. Currently, they average just two or three.

The Kuna hold jurisdiction over the access to the resources of their territorial waters, one of the rights secured in their revolution, and along with control comes responsibility — responsibility to reverse what Panamanian ecologist Jorge Ventocilla refers to as "submarine deforestation." But halting all lobstering was viewed as an extreme measure, since the catches supported the families of the *langosteros* and represented one of the staples of the Kuna's gastronomy.

To combat this tragedy of the commons, the Kuna sought to uncover a balance between conservation and cash: beginning with inspections of all lobsters to be sold, they mandated that the creatures must be of reproductive age. The Kuna have long realized the value of education and have accompanied the regulation with a campaign of awareness, which is why in every island I visited in the archipelago, I saw posters commanding "Let it grow," in both Kuna and Spanish, depicting pictures of spiny lobsters with rulers alongside them. And thus the trade has been carefully continuing.

In fact, with half a day's notice, Nali's café on Narganá would gladly fix me up a spiny lobster dinner, as other cooks on other Kuna Yala islands had done for me in the past. Before this journey, however, my own investigation into the decline of the lobster population had troubled me. Maybe I was contributing to the demise of a creature whose only culpability is being delicious. Especially when lightly salted and drizzled with fried garlic and vegetable oil.

My stomach and brain went about resolving their differences by sending me on a mission to discover how the conservation projects were going. After asking islanders if they knew where I might find Smithsonian Tropical Research Institute biologist Arcadio Castillo, who has been analyzing the habits and populations of the spiny lobsters hiding in the reefs of the comarca, I was directed to the island of Niadup, an hour east of Narganá.

Niadup is a small island where racks of jawbones from wild peccaries hang against the cane reeds of hunter's houses, and a glance down into the hole of an over-the-water outhouse is akin to peering into a colorful aquarium. I met Arcadio across the table at the island's highest structure, the two-story concrete restaurant.

Dressed casually in shorts and a polo shirt, he answered with surprising seriousness and swiftness. Using Niadup as an example of the current vigilant situation, he pointed out that earlier in the day, all three of the island's lobstermen searched for eight hours each, holding their breath as long as they could on each dive, and only pulled in a combined 10 lobsters, about a third of the haul for a single *langostero* from decades past. The lucky, grinning *langostero* who pulled in six of those 10 had been celebrating a bonus of the day over a few beers at the café.

The man's fortunate haul would have to suffice for a long while, because in just two days, starting March 1, one of the newest conservation efforts would begin: a three-month ban on selling lobsters to help boost the population.   The ban, or *veda*, was approved by the Kuna's General Congress and has been levied in addition to the minimum length requirement.

The enforcement of the laws, performed by the Kuna themselves, has been strict.   Arcadio showed me the island's lobster log, completed in longhand by the inspector at the airport, which detailed every lobster sold, including its sex, the family selling the lobster, and its size, which must measure 8 centimeters from its eyes to the start of its tail.

But Arcadio has gone even further to safeguard the Kuna underwater treasure. The project sent several Kuna lobstermen to Mexico, whose coastline harbors the same species of lobster, and whose lobstermen enjoy a larger catch. In addition to two distinct bans on lobstering, spanning a combined seven months out of the year, the Mexicans have built what are called "little Cuban houses." While sounding like a rustic program to surreptitiously foment a Fidel-inspired revolution, they are actually concrete pools built onto the seabed to cultivate young lobsters and protect them from predators—other than humans, that is.   Cuban fishermen introduced the technique to Mexico in the 1960s and the latter has enjoyed improved lobster hauls since. Soon the coasts of Kuna Yala could be dotted with little Cuban houses too.

But for now, during the *veda*, Arcadio's team will be scuba diving around the fragile reefs of Kuna Yala, an activity normally illegal in the province to avoid destruction of the reefs' underwater ecology. The rare and careful dives will soon provide a more accurate assessment of the lobster population to gauge future actions.

It's a big fuss for a little creature, but it's clear to me that the Kuna take the spiny lobster seriously.   And while the lobster projects are in full swing, shellfish lovers may wish to take note that the *veda* also applies to other tragically tasty characters: octopus, conch, and *centollo*, or giant crab. Kuna cooks will still be frying up plenty of jurel and other fish whose populations have remained bountiful, and you can be sure that many *langosteros* will be tossing out fishing lines from their canoes to earn cash for their families in the meantime.

Fishing seems to be the easier line of work anyway. While traditional Kuna fishing, nonetheless, remains a laborious endeavor, since rods are not used and lines are hoisted in by hand (hoping the catch is not large enough to slice open the fisherman's palms with the line), its challenges cannot compare to the daily perils awaiting the lobster diver. Armed with a snorkel mask, fins, a pole noose, and stamina, the Kuna lobsterman dives off of a wooden dugout canoe, a scrawny peel of a boat barely the width of a forearm, and holds his breath for as long as he dares. While sharks have taken lives — and limbs — away from Kuna lobstermen, the chronic effects of the unsympathetic tropical sun must not be overlooked, especially for a caste of fishermen who routinely wear nothing more than Speedos. And don't forget the danger of misjudging the limits of man's ability to starve the body of oxygen while combing the reef, accounting for the lives of 33 Kuna divers in the past 20 years. In other words, it's not about pulling up lobsterpots, a practice that still remains elusive to the *langosteros* of Kuna Yala due to the equipment's substantial investment.

With all the inherent difficulties of lobster diving, why wouldn't the divers trade in their snorkel gear and go fishing instead for the entire year? Back at Narganá, I met up with Isidro, the lobster inspector of the island and a diver himself, who met me under the nautical props, plastic and endearingly kitschy, hanging off the ceiling of Nali's café. He was still toting a bucket that contained his day's hoard of crustaceans, antennae aflutter, when he pointed out two reasons vouching for the popularity of lobstering. The first is money. On a good day, a lobsterman can earn $80, whereas a fisherman cannot usually earn more than $30. And the other reason: risk tends to attract and cultivate bravado. The thrill, for some, makes the trade what it is. Clearly something about the calling kept Isidro happy, for instead of nursing a stiff, tired glaze after diving for eight hours, he glowed with, what I can only describe as, a lobsterman's high.

"I have a map in my head," he stated, not without pride. There are reefs that harbor more lobsters than others, and only experience can assist the diver. Aside from the occasional and unexpected spat between divers over the same lucky spot, the locations remain a secret. A secret that yielded him four large lobsters that day.

The disoriented creatures, crowned with thick front antennae — instead of the large claws of their cousins from the New England coast — sulked backward into their curled tails below the table. Isidro offered to sell me one for dinner, a choice all too easy since his wife worked at the café and would cook it up. With just two days remaining in the Kuna lobstering season, I made my selection.

When Melanie and I returned for dinner, Isidro's wife brought out the spiny lobster, cooked, in fact, with salt, fried garlic, and vegetable oil — the flavor of income, the flavor of conservation, the flavor of tradition.

* * *

At last, we met with an occasion to observe the reenactment of the Kuna Revolution, albeit the circumstances were regrettable. A woman from Niadup had passed away on the anniversary of the revolution, leading to the respectful rescheduling of the island's ceremony a few days later. Nonetheless, the island's *saila* had encouraged us to attend.

Pepito motored us back to Niadup early. The islanders were still setting up their cane reed stage, but already the heat from the morning sun pressed down upon our heads like a vice. The third movement of Mozart's Sonata in A trickled from a tinny tape player and onto villagers leisurely collecting in front of the stage. Grandmothers shrouded in handkerchief bonnets crossed their arms and chewed on tobacco pipes. Behind them, seared red faces of albinos, prevalent in the tight gene pool of the comarca, poked out from the open-air windows.

The island felt no need to hasten the festivities. Niadup had planned an all-day re-enactment featuring the events that led up to the revolution, for the morning, and the lightning insurrection after a siesta.

Men and women alike reddened their cheeks with *achiote* and wore t-shirts splashed with embroideries of the Kuna's traditional four-sided symbol — what coincidentally appears to be a swastika. The symbol was derived independently from a common design on molas, and not, as some still believe, from the Third Reich (although to an outsider, it was, at first, alarming to watch children frolicking about with the bright red emblem painted on their faces).

Young Kuna men in the khaki and camouflage of Panamanian police uniforms sucked from a bottle of 70-proof *seco* — clear Panamanian cane liquor — and lit firecrackers from their cigarettes to get into character. Wooden stocks, a prop appearing realistic enough for serving punishment, sat beside children weaving quivers out of palm leaves. The tape player then groaning out a distorted Mozart's Symphony in G minor, the ceremony began with a short march around the island whose huts had been burned to the ground during an early skirmish with the Panamanian colonial forces 80 years ago.

The *seco*-sweating policemen patrolled the street in between the onlookers past the village's new queen, crowned yesterday. She exuded her modern statement of regality with a tiara, capris, and a pink Brooklyn t-shirt (Brooklyn used to be named King's County, after all). "The colonial rule oppressed our traditions," continued the grievances of the event's announcer through a boxy microphone fanning out his somber circus bark, as the police let loose their rubber truncheons upon actors successively posing as bathers, plantain carriers, and delousing buddies. "The *colonos* robbed us of our turtles..."

"They wanted to exterminate the Kuna race," a villager drilled into my ear as we watched half the troupe beating the other half. Instead of utilizing the static confines of the stage, the action sprawled across the width of the street and drew staggered giggles from the onlookers peering in from all sides, melding performer and observer together.

Soon the pain of high noon hastened the end of the morning's theatrics. I had received permission from the *sailas* to take pictures of the event and, to give gratitude, I bought beers for some of the actors and the announcer, for the island had not prepared any *inna* for the event. The announcer, sweating below a baseball-style cap embroidered with the Kuna symbol, took a liking to my generosity and insisted on half a dozen more rounds for himself, ensuring intermission would be unrushed.

Foot traffic became sparse, as the sun sent most of the villagers under their thatched roofs. A caged iguana marked the entrance to one such abode. The sight may have been odd—and perhaps illegal—in one of the deforested parts of the country, but iguanas still remain plentiful in the trees of Kuna Yala's well-preserved jungle.

The vigilant captive sat up above its meal of flowers scattered on the bottom of its cage so endearingly that I asked a girl reclining in a nearby hammock what they had named the lizard. She ripped into laughter. A woman emerged from the threshold of the house, answering my inquiry by swinging another iguana — this one limp, pale, and not quite integral — from the end of her arm, her other hand wrapped around the handle of a knife. Alas, I had once again failed to tell pet from meat in the rural folds of the isthmus.

Alight with beer and *seco* (and for some, a little iguana stew), the troupe returned to finish its saga of a celebration. With carved wooden props, they acted out the offensive strategies of the revolution that secured their autonomy, felling the colonial police with axes and the police's own guns. And, in the end, despite the actors toasting victory with — ironically — Panamanian beer, the land of Mother Earth still thrives under the attentive protection of her children.

8.
To House a Dictator

A NEAT SPINE OF BROKEN GLASS, mortared jagged side up, adorns the top of the concrete wall separating Panama City's Vatican embassy from the traffic gushing down Avenida Balboa. When I approached the entrance, the flourish, only a little above eye-height, seemed to me to be more for urban aesthetics than security; now with a shopping center across the street, the nuncio only has to concern itself with keeping mall rats off papal turf. Recently, however, the same fashionable masonry had successfully divided two camps in one of Latin America's most famous standoffs: George Bush Senior versus Panamanian dictator Manuel Noriega.

I'm talking about the climactic scene of an era of double-dealing spies, slush funds feeding insurgencies and counterinsurgencies, and large amounts of cash discreetly stuffed into noses of airplanes. A car bomb here, a secret White House venture there. It was the stuff of thriller novels.

On Christmas Eve 1989, Noriega, indicted on drug trafficking charges, snuck under the muzzles and fancy war toys of the invading American patrols and dropped into the embassy, his last chance for asylum. But the strongman was no stranger to the invaders. Counterbalancing his 5-foot 6 height and pitted complexion — branding him ever-famously as "pineapple face" — Noriega had been selling intel on Cuba to the United States for over 20 years. At the same time, however, he accumulated an impressive portfolio of authoritarian accomplishments, including money laundering, rape (once in police uniform), election rigging, drug running, firing on demonstrators, corruption, terrorism, press restrictions, and a beheading of a man who knew too much — in other words, just the sort of clever, well-connected powerhouse the CIA has often cultivated (although not as ghastly as other past CIA freelancers, namely Saddam Hussein and Osama Bin Laden).

Unfortunately for Noriega, America had stopped ignoring the strongman's transgressions suspiciously around the time that Noriega refused President Reagan's request for Panama to invade Nicaragua alongside America and overthrow Nicaragua's democratically elected government (the plan was part of Reagan's curiously named "Project Democracy"). Add on the growing anti-drug sentiment across the States, and Noriega had gone from ally to liability. Perhaps Panama would have eventually tossed out Noriega on her own (coups used to be as Panamanian as *arroz con pollo*), but the United States wanted to leave nothing to chance.

The invasion had confined Noriega to watching a blurry television in an upstairs room of the Vatican embassy, an AK-47 under his mattress for a last resort. America, however, needed not turn to lethal methods to extract their man, instead employing a truly modern ballistic: rock music.   Soaking the embassy compound with a storm of decibels (quite the network-friendly, primetime sound byte), the psy-ops team dealt the tiny building a continuous stream of commercial-free programming, including such ditties as The Clash's "I fought the law and the law won." But even this "roaring, mind-bending din," as described by Noriega in his memoirs, did not flush out the dictator. Perhaps the Vatican's own nuncio delivered the more effective tactic, asking Noriega if he wanted to have nuns wash his underwear for the rest of his life.

When the dictator emerged from the Vatican sans-AK-47, the U.S. government would start picking up the tab for his laundry in a Miami prison. He would be convicted of drug trafficking and human rights violations, most of which occurred during the years when he was drawing a CIA paycheck, including the years when Bush Senior was the head of the CIA.

The next day, a Panama City ice cream parlor ran a special on their pineapple flavor.

* * *

Fourteen years later, the security situation at the embassy had reverted to tropical casualness. No guards patrolled the entrance. The gates were open. So why not walk in?

The parking lot within lay blissfully empty and quiet, except for maybe a faint echo of a dictator's last clumsy steps out of the country.

But the echo grew louder and urgently crisper. A guard had appeared from somewhere. "Who are you? You can't enter!"

I thought of concocting a story that I was seeking asylum: the Vatican let in a murdering rapist dictator, so I figured they would accept a humble writer from the States. But I thought against the idea, since if the story went too far, I might end up having nuns wash my underwear for the rest of my life. I offered the truth: I attempted to explain that as a writer I was interested in observing the building where the standoff had occurred. Could I just look around for a minute?

"No." The guard swept through a slow nod. Instead of ushering me out, however, he folded his arms and froze, staring at me as if he were expecting a password. What could it be? Holy Water? Immaculate Conception?

I gave up. I would just have to placate my curiosity with the view of the embassy from the shopping mall's steps across the street.

As I started toward the Avenue, the guard pursued. "Wait. There might be another way to get in," he said. His stare glowed warm and expectant as he simultaneously sent off a few words of adoration in the direction of a passing young woman while managing to help me figure out the password: money. He pushed open the gate with one hand and left the other hand open. "*Rápido*," he remarked.

With its rippled roof and concrete walls slathered in pastel-colored paint, the building could have been an affluent *capitaleño's* weekend house tucked on the lush slopes of the extinct volcano of El Valle, a few hours west of the city. A quaint walkway, partially paved, negotiated past manicured palm tree tufts along the perimeter. The Avenue, cinched behind the glass-topped levee, seemed miles away.

And that was about it. If you are going to run and hide from the world's most powerful military, you might as well choose a place as emphatically serene for your last moments of freedom.

In all its humility, the building claims the distinction of being the place where Panama's destiny had changed in 1990. While there used to be a Panamanian adage "It's not who wins that counts; it's who counts that wins," internal and international observers have ruled all of Panama's presidential elections after Noriega's downfall as fair. And the heads of anti-drug activists have since remained attached to their respective bodies.

As the guard thanked me when I left, I realized that some other forms of Panamanian dealings still remain intact.

9.
The Rumba Emberá

I REALIZED SOMETHING WAS ASKEW when I noticed a large, grunting rodent following me.

It wasn't that I should be alarmed when encountering such a cat-sized animal, an agouti, in the forests of Central America. But why was this normally timid and nocturnal creature scuttling about at noontime so close to a human, its number one predator?

Lucky for him, he was a pet. It is illegal to hunt game in the jungle around Parara Puru, an Emberá village of 57 people on the banks of the Chagres River. Most of the land surrounding the river was declared a national park by the government in 1984 to protect the Panama Canal watershed, since the Chagres provides water necessary for the operation of the Canal. As a result, the park is still home to tropical game, unlike many other parts of Panama that have been stripped of the forest and its erosion-fighting power to accommodate crops and pasture.

Despite being traditional hunters prowling the forest of the isthmus with spears, as their ancestors have done for centuries, and despite the bounty leaping around them, the villagers had to forfeit their main form of sustenance and begin viewing the tasty animal behind me as a mascot. Since long before the arrival of *conquistadores*, an Emberá chief would decide to move his community if the area's fauna concentration became thin, in order to allow nature to recover the animal population of the area. The cycle continued to sustain. Now, with the arrival of fixed boundaries, land titles, and a loss of more than half the forest coverage of 100 years ago, many Emberá communities have moved to either avoid infringing Panamanian settlements or dangerous guerilla activities near the Colombian border (a location where many Emberá still live). Sometimes they relocate to places that do not allow hunting—or even substantially sized agriculture plots, as is the case with Parara Puru—in exchange for securing a natural forest setting. The nomadic Emberá have had to adapt.

What does a community with a rich tradition of hunting do when squeezed out of one homeland and not allowed to engage in traditional sustenance in the other? The people of Parara Puru neither conceded defeat nor spilled blood, as did some of the other native peoples of the Americas when the colonial plague struck. The community, instead, decided to leverage their proximity to Panama City and entice as many visitors that could fit into a dugout canoe to visit their beautiful piece of the globe, still rich with jaguars, howler monkeys, and foliage sagging under its own ripeness.

Earlier in the day, Romero, a village resident turned nature guide, led me on a hike upstream along the riverbank—most likely along what used to be a hunting path. "My grandfather was the first to move here," he announced, his thumbs stuck in bands of yellow beads slung over his shoulders. His grandfather chose to move the community to avoid encroachment of the Panamanian settlements at their old location 14 years ago by settling on the Chagres River just upstream of Lake Alajuela, an artificial lake created in 1935, to provide more water for the functioning of the Panama Canal's locks.

At the end of the 20-minute hike, a waterfall roared and beckoned. Wasting no time, Romero dove straight down into the pool that collected in front of the two stories of tumbling refreshment and then disappeared into the apparent shallowness of the water. He emerged and climbed to the top of the waterfall, sending off a fulfilling chuckle taunt.

He needed not take off his shoes, since he hiked the path without any. The rainy season had ravaged the path into a shoe-swallowing mud romp anyway, yet still reserved a few swatches of jutting rocks for unexpected, flesh-scraping excitement. He also hadn't any need to change into a bathing suit — his skirt-like bead wrap served the purpose. I, on the other hand, did not have my bathing suit handy, but after the hike through the clam-juice air of a tropical late morning, I wasn't going to be denied. I jumped in anyway and joined a few *sábalo* (shad) and *sabaleta* scouting just below the surface of the cool, frothy water that would soon float a vessel across the Canal. "Those fish taste good, too," remarked Romero. The village is still permitted to fish, and why not? If they don't catch the fish in the river, the fish would just end up getting sucked into the ballast of a cargo ship instead.

Back at one of the village's common buildings, the villagers were frying up a different kind of aquatic dweller, tilapia, caught from the lake. It is unlikely that tilapia fishing will ever be banned, since tilapia was introduced to Latin America from its native Africa decades ago for its commercial value and has been zestfully plundering the food supply of the native species ever since.

It is also the supposed fish that Jesus served everyone when he delivered his Sermon on the Mount. Unlike most biblical fables, this one remains credible because tilapia is a hearty, fast-growing fish that breeds early and often. He shouldn't have had trouble securing a comfortably adequate supply for the gathering and, since tilapia meat is juicy and tasty, I'm sure the offerings made Jesus a celebrity with the crowd. Tasty enough, in fact, to help launch a religion in his name. What a fish.

Well, the meek haven't inherited the earth, but at least we can enjoy a good meal. The fish chunks were tumbling through bubbly oil in a pot above a fogon, a traditional three-pronged wood fire used liberally throughout the electricity-free patches of the isthmus. I glanced upward to find that lunch was cooking under a roof made up of layers of palm leaves. Asphyxiation was not a worry because, with a thatched roof that has been layered properly, smoke works its way out, while rain does not enter — brilliant, simple, and still effective.

The elderly cook, illiterate but penning volumes with her heartening calmness, handed me the crispy tilapia and a few fried plantains in a serving cradle made of a folded up *bijao* leaf, the same banana-like leaf they use to fashion cups that reliably carry drinking water during hikes in the forest. The meal offered me an abundance of opportunities to practice my pronunciation of *biabua*, "thank you" in the Emberá language. The tongue is spoken by the estimated 15,000 Emberá in Panama and western Colombia, yet remains absent from any government-sponsored elementary school.

Up the bank, well past the dark, hole-style outhouses — not very conducive to a magazine rack — chickens scoured the hillside along the manicured grounds of fruit trees and underneath the raised-platform pole houses. No fences here, not even chicken wire.

Halfway up the hill, past a cacao tree sprouting a few demure red pods, I found Milenio, the village's ample-bellied medicine man, his vibrant skin divulging only a few of his 70-odd years. He has cultivated a medicinal plant garden that he enjoys showing to visitors as much as a suburbanite fancies shuffling his guests around his cherry tomatoes in the backyard. But what good is a cherry tomato when pitted against one of Milenio's plants that can reverse the effects of a potentially deadly snakebite? Or reduce fever? Or clean your teeth as effectively as toothpaste? Without any health care facility in the village, the villagers still rely on some of the same medicinal plants as they have for centuries.

But there was no doubt about the era in which the village lived. The metal pot used for lunch was from the same discount array of cookware I'd seen at department stores in the capital. A glance around the houses on the hillside revealed clotheslines draped with t-shirts and other Western articles of clothing, items that presently could not be found on any of the villagers, but there was little wonder as to who was going to wear them as soon as all the visitors had left. An American flag, a gift from a tourist, dangled off a railing under a thatch roof porch. Everyone spoke fluent Spanish. The motor hanging off the dugout canoe cut the trip across the lake down to a quaint 20 minutes. For five days a week, an instructor from the interior province of Veraguas lives in the village and teaches standard subjects in the schoolhouse. The village has placed one dauntless barefoot in each world and doesn't seem intent on giving up claim to either side.

Since locating each one of the dozens of medicinal plants in the forest would prove a cumbersome endeavor, Milenio's well-weeded botanical garden was grown at the village for the benefit of tourists. (I'm sure the villagers take advantage of the convenience as well if they need a remedy for a damning headache. Who wants to lumber around for an hour in the jungle to locate the appropriate plant while the temples are throbbing?) As a true testament to the modernity of the Emberá culture, however, one of their medicinal plants provides the cure for gonorrhea, a bacteria originally gifted by the *conquistadores*.

Surprisingly absent, however, was a church of any kind. Missionaries from many flavors of Christianity can usually detect an unconverted village from thousands of miles away and, in fact, many indigenous villages in Panama, no matter how small, already boast one or more competing places of Christian worship. But Christianity is one export of the Western world that Parara Puru has, thus far, left at the boat launch.

Where Christianity has remained foreign, consumption culture has established a beachhead. Gustavo, my guide from Panama City and frequent visitor of Parara Puru, told me that the children from the village often ask him what gifts he is going to bring to the village next. One asked for a game of jax. Another requested a Barbie doll. "I feel a little like Santa Claus," Gustavo remarked.

The afternoon's burden of rain sent us all for cover under another common building built for visitors—the largest in the village—lined with tables displaying village-made crafts. Emberá baskets claim a history of household use, but now more intricate pieces are created and sold for cash so the villagers can purchase staples such as gasoline, cooking oil, and rice.   A basket craftsman, clad only in a bright orange loincloth, fetched a beaded headband and placed it over his short, geometric, Panama City-style haircut and spread his arms over his wares like a blackjack dealer.   Carrying the cash he collected for his artisan works appeared to present a challenge, save some secret pocket sewn into nouveau Emberá loincloths.

Turning another traditional practice into a moneymaker, a village woman offered to paint my arm with intricate geometrical designs using *jagua*, blue-black ink created from cooking the immature fruit of the genipa tree.   The fruit is no stranger to the Western world, however.   In a boldly humble corporate maneuver, Aveda, a U.S.-based cosmetic corporation that uses a blue pigment derived from genipa for some if its products, decided to compensate the native tribes in Brazil who helped the company identify the fruit and its uses.

Jagua's uses span beyond aesthetics; the Emberá also use *jagua* as a sunscreen. "It's also a natural mosquito repellent," she added, her delicate painting motions undisturbed by her curious child fidgeting at her side.   If anyone knows how to repel mosquitoes, it's the Emberá. Since both sexes, until recently, have spent centuries topless save a few bands of decorative beads — not to mention that their pole houses are built with permanently open ventilation to combat the tropical heat — I'll trust they have learned a thing or two about keeping the biting air force at bay.

The rain remained unchallenged, however.   The villagers made the best of the deluge by congregating under the common roof and rounding up their arsenal of handmade musical instruments.   A troupe of female dancers, led by a teenager playing a hand drum, began stomping and swinging in a smooth circle, while a small child stood obliviously in the middle, caught up in the whirl of activity she would join in a few years.

The band tapped, scraped, and shook out a tight rhythm, trumping the static drone of the downpour.   As a percussionist, I was impressed with the rich range of sounds eked from a two-sided drum, a turtle shell, gourd rattles, a scratchy guiro, and a bamboo flute. Perhaps the aural quality owed itself to the fact that one head of the drum had been fashioned from the skin of a male deer and the other a female — "It sounds better that way," they insisted.   Joining the lineup of musicians was none other than Milenio, the local medicine man, who not only possesses a cure for the Clap, but also lays down a mean beat on the turtle shell.

The Embera have created many dances to celebrate the elements in their environment that have sustained them, one that the leader called "el trapiche" (a wooden device which crushes the juice out of cane reeds), and others for various tropical animals that used to appear on the menu.   Since their arrival at the river 14 years ago, they added another celebratory number to their repertoire: the Rumba Emberá.   You might acquire the impression that they are celebrating the regular arrival of Santa's sleigh—er, I mean motorized canoes—from Panama City.

Hunkered down under the thatch roof, several villagers asked me to teach them a few basic English-language greetings. In exchange, they demonstrated some of the basic maneuvers in carving the tagua nut, a curious plum-sized fruit that resembles ivory. But the tagua tree is much more prolific than tusked mammals. Each year, a single tagua palm tree produces the same amount of ivory as an elephant. "You can eat the nuts when they're young," Condor, the craftsman with the aforementioned haircut, pointed out. "When they're young, they're soft. Tastes like coconut."

The mature nuts used to be harvested for the carving of buttons and chess pieces before plastic was invented. For about the past 30 years, the Embera have capitalized on the nuts' resemblance to ivory (which is why the nuts are also called "vegetable ivory") by fastidiously whittling the nuts into sculptures of forest animals and reptiles. "Try it," Condor insisted, handing me a dry nut ready for carving and a thin metal blade. The medium was soft enough to concede a small gouge, but hard enough for me to gain considerable respect for the artists of the village who spent days—and sometimes weeks—on each piece while tweaking each claw of a curled up, 4-centimeter iguana. And visitors can forget scoring a cutesy, smiling trinket. The works on display feature accurate anatomical details and colors worthy of a nerdy zoologist.

I examined such a nut featuring a pair of turtle hatchlings peering out of their shells. "I cut myself here while making that one," the artist announced, pointing to a fresh, pink scar across the meat of his left palm.

The nut's petite size is no obstacle for the artists. One of them joined two nuts seamlessly with glue, capturing all the action of a paca—a rodent resembling an agouti but with rows of white spots—munching on wild maize. "We eat those, you know," stated a girl (who was the lead dancer), observing my interest in the paca or, more eloquently, in Spanish, *conejo pintado*—painted rabbit.

"What kind of flavor does paca have?" I asked.

"Very rich!" she answered without hesitation. I don't think their pet agouti has anything to worry about, since the paca, from my non-scientific survey of over a dozen people from various parts of rural Panama, is the tastiest critter in the bush by an almost unanimous vote. The only dissenter reserved the superlative for sea turtle eggs but, technically, they're not quite critters yet (and they're not found in the bush—rather on the beach). Offering creative recipes for every isthmian creature from the wild peccary to the quetzal, the Canal Zone culinary mentor Gladys Graham, in her 1947 work titled *Tropical Cooking: a Handbook of Tropical Foods*, tantalizingly described paca meat as "white and sweet." She says, "Roast him whole, stuck with cloves, and basted with orange juice, and your family and guests will want to desert meat markets and take to the woods for provender."

If Graham had written the book nowadays, the opus would have ended up considerably skimpier, since paca and most others whose loins she stewed with care ("everything but the buzzard!" she lovingly wrote) are currently forbidden to eat, unless part of a regulation program. How do the villagers, even ones who were infants when the park was created, know the flavor of this coy, spotted creature?

Now I bet you're ringing your hands, cackling about the fact that I've just spent a few thousand words defending the village's restraint on hunting, and now we have caught them with the proverbial paca over the fire. It would now be appropriate to point out that several communities of Emberá live inside the

Chagres National Park and, wherever Emberá are, there are record numbers of rainforest fauna (relative to the rest of Panama). If the villages take an animal occasionally, they have done it in a way that is both sustainable and respectable. Good for them.

And since Lake Alajuela not only supplies 40 percent of the water used by the Panama Canal, but also drinking water for Colón and Panama City, the protection of the erosion-fighting trees around the lake sustains much more than the village. With their history of living harmoniously with the rainforest, I can't think of a more appropriate caretaker.

10.
Temptations

ROTTING RATIONS WERE RUNNING LOW. Fevers were running high. The year was 1503, an era when cartographers still painted sea monsters on their maps.

Mariners clinging to a fleet of worm-eaten vessels disembarked onto a swatch of jungle in search of a route to the other side of the planet. Even though the people native to the land informed the crew that another ocean awaited just a 10-day hike to the south, the admiral lost his taste for exploration and, instead, began feverishly collecting ornamental "mirrors" that the natives wore around their necks. The admiral, Christopher Columbus, was sailing on his fourth and last voyage across the Atlantic.

Despite his crew feverishly bailing out his ships with pots and kettles, Columbus lost all four vessels, so devoured by sea worms that he referred to the hulls as honeycombs. Two sank into the waters of what is now the Caribbean coast of Panama. Boats or no boats, ocean passage or none, the Genoan explorer still felt that he had validated his journey. Why? The isthmian "mirrors" he collected were fashioned from gold.

And thus the craze began, in its entire antisocial splendor. Soon Panama City cropped up and served as the Pacific terminus of a supply route carrying Spanish colony gold, mostly from mines at which the Amerindians were enslaved, to the Atlantic side and back to Europe. The intoxicating scent of the spoils attracted the often-romanticized Welsh privateer Henry Morgan, who ravaged the city in 1671, torturing gold out of whoever hadn't escaped by boat (how romantic). The California gold rush of 1849 reawakened the frenzy, calling upon Panama City as the port for transporting hopeful American panners by boat to the new West Coast state. Shortly after the Panama Railroad began cutting across the isthmus in 1850, panners itching for riches paid the Railroad for however far the partially completed tracks would take them.

What has become of the city's nugget lust? Jungle reclaimed the mines many generations ago, and tourists and Colón's Free Zone employees replaced panners on the Panama Railroad, but in the capital's Cinco de Mayo plaza, I sensed echoes of the pursuit trickling out from the Museo Antropológico Reina Torres de Araúz, housed in what used to be the Railroad's old terminal station. The museum's gold room not only contains a few gold mirrors, so coveted by Columbus, but also requires all persons — guides and visitors alike — to sign in and show identification before entry (my passport sufficed). Such measures discourage a repeat of a heist — believed to be an inside job — that hauled away almost 300 gold and ceramic treasures in early 2003. While 90 percent was recovered a few months later, the other 10 percent is assumed to have entered America's black market for antiquities, satisfying the most discerning trophy-hunting conquistadors of today.

And speaking of satisfaction, on a corner wall of the gold room hangs an ink print illustrating the practice of Amerindians fulfilling a Spaniard's material desires by pinning him down and pouring melted gold into his mouth.

Centuries after greed was answered with such poetic punishment, a much ampler variety of allurements and endeavors has seized the Panama City of today, as evident from a stroll southward from the Cinco de Mayo plaza. A few jewelry stores dotting the city's pedestrian-only street Central Peatonal offer only a token whimper of the city's past gold trade—the stores' glistening offerings lost among $5 cooking pots and plastic toys spilled onto the sidewalk, fresh produce vendors, and a kaleidoscopic train wreck of every culture on the isthmus. Laden with bags of fruit, Ngöbe women in bright turquoise dresses stroll past fast food restaurants. Campesinos from the interior of the country remove their straw hats to sop their foreheads with handkerchiefs pulled from pockets of guayabera shirts. Women from Kuna Yala, donning traditional puffy-shouldered dresses and studs through pierced septums, chuckle and sit under the arms of their husbands or boyfriends, some of whom are Latinos—a combination not terribly popular on the more traditional Kuna islands.

The most pronounced institution on the Peatonal, however, is also a most welcome solution to the city's climate: the *chicha*. Unlike the fermented *chichas* of the Andes, the refreshing drink known in Panama as the *chicha* is non-alcoholic, yet that is just about the only trait Panamanian *chichas* share with each other. Blended with ice, sugar, powdered milk, or any combination, cups of *chichas* take advantage of the variety of tropical fruits grown on the isthmus: silky guanabana; frothy pineapple; tamarind, its acidity tamed by sugar; the murky green pleasure of sugar cane juice, unfortunately seasonal; papaya with milk, smooth and creamy. And they're much more preferable to molten gold on a hot day.

Grains also produce tasty *chichas*. Sadly, my favorite 25-cent *chicha* stall near the Cinco de Mayo Plaza had run out of *avena*, a drink of oats, sugar, milk, and cinnamon. In search of a surrogate,

I patrolled the Central Peatonal, weaving among an army of sweating, hand-painted pushcarts hawking 25-cent cups of a sweet corn and milk drink known as *chichéme* and beverage combinations such as *arroz con piña*, or rice and pineapple.

With so many blenders gyrating, how does one decide?   By choosing one at a time, of course.   Melanie and I selected a large shake made of the *naranjilla* fruit, its flavor summoning pineapple, lime, and green apple.   But the equatorial sun blasted on, requiring further reinforcements, guaranteeing we'd engorge ourselves with *chichas* as fast as we could sweat them out.   Soon I added a shake of *borojó*, a tart fruit that has been enjoyed by the Emberá people of Eastern Panama and Western Colombia for centuries.   This wonderfully tangy treat may lose some of its appeal if you fixate on the fact that *borojó* means "head fruit" in the Emberá language, since the fruit ripens to the shape of a smooth noggin. The label may seem too appropriate when the fruit is whipped up with milk and sugar, yielding a drab, quivering spume that awards a completely new meaning to gray matter.

In this modern crossroads of culture, a multiplicity of languages jumps into the blender as well.   Even though I ordered in Spanish, the manager of the chicha stall used English when she barked "Fifty cents in change" to the young cashier. The cashier stared at the register with frozen iguana eyes. "Panama should have been bilingual long ago! I know. I am Panamanian," the manager commented to me after she translated for her cashier. (Perhaps she should send her cashier to the Smithsonian Institute's research center on Barro Colorado Island in the Panama Canal, where everything from scientific lectures to cafeteria announcements uses English, the lingua franca of the island.) While the Peatonal remains more of a *capitaleño* hangout than a tourist attraction, the shop owner should not anguish, because many vendors on Central Peatonal demonstrate, at least, a superficial English proficiency, especially in nearby stores named TOP GOLD and the ever-popular bilingual hybrid ROPA CITY.

At $1.50, the *borojó* concoction was the most I had paid for a *chicha*. While the fruit is rich in protein and even phosphorous — unusual for a fruit grown in tropical soil — the vendors justify the extra expense from the fact that *borojó* is considered an aphrodisiac. I'm confident, however, that just about anything could be labeled an aphrodisiac if pimped by the proper marketing campaign. I don't think we're too far off from the announcement that a proprietary mixture of used antifreeze and lima beans will have the neighbors pounding on your walls (and now available in an easily dissolvable packet).

After I finished off the last of my large "head fruit" shake, I did not discern any increase in my appetite for flesh, despite walking around a city whose fashion czars ruthlessly mandate a caravan of curve-clung attire, with its proud panty lines afoot, and prouder sideline praise ablaze.

The Central Peatonal harbors an assemblage of benches where you can wrap yourself in the parade of fashion, while the bells of *raspado* carts jingle their way over each cobblestone. The *chicha's* main competitors, *raspados* (snow cone carts) combat the heat with an array of sugary syrups and condensed milk for a quarter. One *raspa'o* vendor fashioned his cart in the shape of a *diablo rojo* bus complete with the obligatory trimmings: a rainbow of light bulbs on the hood, airbrushed artwork enlivening the sides, and dual exhaust pipes serving as pushcart handles. All the while, the real *diablos rojos*, with hand-painted monikers such as DANGEROUS THING and PUSSY BREAKER, remained safely above the pedestrian street while they expelled husky diesel flatulence and circled the plaza like pacing bullies. Predictably, bus driving in Panama is a male dominated vocation.

But in Panama, power is by no means limited to those with a Y chromosome — that is, if you claim the right pedigree. We passed an assortment of graffiti comparing the last president, Mireya Moscoso, to a fascist. Besides risking vandalism charges, the graffiti's author would have most likely kept himself fastidiously anonymous to escape Moscoso's penchant for blackballing — and even jailing — those who criticized her. "Well dressed" would probably serve as a more apt description of Moscoso, the widow of one of Panama's ex-presidents, since she is now being investigated for spending more than $1,600 a week of public funds on clothing and jewelry for herself in a country where the median weekly income is less than $50. She replied to the charges with "I couldn't walk around ragged."

Rounding out the Peatonal's food parade, tables piled with apples and puffy grapes imported from Chile vied valiantly against the street's array of fast food vendors. Many of the latter offerings had already been fried an undisclosed number of days ago and were obsequiously courting bacteria under bulb-lit showcase boxes: musty miniature vaudeville acts that should have been cancelled.

Plaza Santa Ana caps the southern end of the Central Peatonal with a column of shoeshine stations, each with a roof to deny hazards of the sun and pigeons' digestive by-products alike. The spines of the stations themselves were striped with varying amounts of shoe polish depending on the shiner's boredom level. As the shiners earned a dollar per customer, the much better attended domino tables in between the stations shook free whatever greenbacks remained.

Across the plaza, the waitresses of café Coca Cola were shuffling out plates of roast chicken with rice and guandu peas. A newspaper seller, meandering among the tables with three popular titles stacked onto his head like a kebab, dug coins out of his ear — the Panamanian vendor's change purse — with one hand and slipped out a piece of the kebab with the other, providing paper and change to his customer in one move. A mother sent her 5-year-old boy into the restaurant to beg for money. "To eat," he had been programmed to say.

Diablos rojos, led by one called KICKING ASES (sic), resumed plowing their airbrushed snouts through the streets outside café Coca Cola. Slowed by milk-mixed *chichas*, however, we decided we would return to our hotel and treat ourselves to a $1.50 taxi ride in a cab lacking back seatbelts — in other words, the average Panama City taxi. BENDECIDO (blessed) read the window of a bus that gunned around another bus next to us, all to score a quarter from the next waiting fare, a competition which the Panamanian daily *La Prensa* refers to as the "suicide race." The sport highlights a main difference between Panama City's public buses and, say, America's. In Panama City, each bus is privately owned and, thus, when routes overlap, the incentive of profit turns the streets into a joust of 12-ton chariots. (As this book goes to press, plans have been announced to replace the owner-operated buses with a monopoly.) Just the week before, a *diablo rojo* rammed a pedestrian who was crossing the street and finished him off under its wheels, creating a photo-op the city's tabloid papers gleefully enlarged across their front pages. A seatbelt in the cab's back seat would have been a nice touch, I thought.

With such a storm of commerce, you might be inclined to believe that Panama City has swapped its gold trade for something newer — *chichas*, or perhaps used transmissions for discarded American vehicles. But the cabbie offered his own unsolicited answer when a woman complying with current fashion leisurely passed us on the sidewalk, her sheer top confessing the fit of her brassiere, drawing the cabbie's head out of the window like a jack-in-the-box. A whistle shot out of his grin. His eyes bounced back toward me and he announced, "*That* is

Panama City!" Melanie's presence did not seem to crimp his sentiments. Somehow, she remained in good humor.

As we entered the neighborhood of El Cangrejo, our destination approached, but never quite arrived. Three young women, tightly sheathed in club-ready outfits, were waiting for a cab about 40 feet ahead of where we had wanted to be dropped off. The cabbie punched the brakes in front of the trio instead. This was our stop too, apparently. As he waved the girls into the taxi, I could have passed him a rotting avocado for the cab fare, and I'm sure he wouldn't have noticed.

He drove off, turning out of the window for what I thought was going to be an apology, but instead he thanked me in a quick cackle for the luck I had apparently brought to him, his tongue a flag flapping in victory. Another fortune hunter finds his gold.

11.
Both Friend and Food

GREEN IGUANAS WEAR MANY HATS. These unassuming reptiles play roles as tourist attractions, pets, and endangered species. However, their role as the main course for dinner is, ironically, providing Panama with a vehicle for the species' conservation.

Iguanas have appeared on menus in Central America for thousands of years, but the species' existence only began to be threatened over the last century as a consequence of excessive hunting and destruction of its habitat to make room for cattle and other agricultural cogs in a cash economy. However, scarcity hasn't quelled the Panamanian's traditional practice of entering the forest with a slingshot and leaving with a "free-range" iguana. With high protein and low fat content, iguanas, which are herbivores, have provided many a family with a fresh, healthy, natural meal. Iguana eggs, a rich, creamy treat, allegedly cure various ailments, once you find a way through the tough, leathery shells.

Balancing the conservation of a species, a regular supply of a customary meal, and income for farmers has never been a simple task. In the 1980s, biologist Dagmar Werner tackled the complex challenge by launching a project in Panama to evaluate the viability of raising iguanas in captivity for food and profit. She soon moved her operation to nearby Costa Rica in order to take advantage of a more nurturing political and economic climate. Despite initial successes, however, the Costa Rica project, including a restaurant serving iguana burgers to promote its cause, recently and unexpectedly closed its doors.

Today, Panama is giving the idea a second chance. Nestled in a park in the watershed of the Panama Canal, ANCON (the Spanish acronym for Panama's National Association for the Conservation of Nature) scientists at the 60-hectare Rio Cabuya Agroforestry Farm have been spearheading a program to teach campesinos how to raise their own iguanas as a sustainable food source. While profits are understandably on the minds of the participating farmers, the primary goal of the project, at least at first, is to keep the campesinos from hunting the threatened creature in the wild.

While poaching wild iguanas is illegal in Panama, little government-funded monitoring actually occurs — and conservationists in Panama have frequently encountered impediments. This lack of oversight triggered a recent decision by the Convention on International Trade in Endangered Species (CITES) that recommends sanctions on all of Panama's CITES-listed exports of both flora and fauna, explicitly due to the government's failure to adopt legislation protecting the country's species in danger of extinction.

Even at the agroforestry site itself, setbacks occur. "Poachers sometimes raid the park and steal a few of our iguanas," explained ANCON Expedition's Rick Morales, as we followed the life cycle of iguanas hatched and raised in the ground's caged housing. The facilities appeared modest and improvised — intentionally — to mimic the availability of whatever building supplies may be lying around any farm in Panama: scrap sheet metal, chicken wire, and spare lumber.

The idea is simple. The project lends campesinos a pair of adult iguanas at no cost and provides tutelage on housing, guarding, and feeding them. In protective captivity, around 95 percent of the 35 or so eggs per clutch will survive. This stands in abrupt contrast to the about 5 percent success rate in the wild, where eggs helplessly succumb to the hunger of ants, snakes, and other natural predators. At six months, adolescent iguanas, virtually predator-free, are either released into the campesinos' trees for future easy-access meals, or they are kept in a larger shelter. After 18 months, the campesinos can swap their breeding iguanas for another pair. To uphold their end of the deal, the campesinos must return 20 percent of the iguanas to the wild. They can sell or eat the rest. The mathematics, in principle, tell us that the forest gains more of a threatened species, the campesinos gain the opportunity to legally eat a traditional meal without hunting in the wild, and only the snakes lose (but don't worry; snakes still have plenty to eat).

So, how successful has the project been? Our search for answers led Rick and me back to the Panama City office of ANCON biologist Augusto Gonzalez, who, for the past 12 years, has been managing the iguana-farming project. According to Gonzalez, the accomplishments of the project varied with the diverse Panamanian geography. "So far, in the Canal watershed area, the participating farms have achieved little," he conceded. Whereas iguanas are threatened throughout Panama, populations in various provinces have been unevenly affected, following uneven patterns of hunting and deforestation. In the watershed of the Panama Canal, the iguana population has suffered less than in other parts of the country, hence the watershed's campesinos do not want to pay for feeding and raising something that they can readily — albeit illegally — catch for free in the wild.

Some iguana farms backfired.   A few would-be iguana ranchers, in the course of protecting and raising the creatures, found the iguana's curtain-like dewlaps and distinguished stares too endearing to eat them, even extending the attachment by giving the creatures names.   Those campesinos could not bear releasing the reptiles into a bordering tree, lest "Paquito" end up on a skewer over a neighbor's barbecue pit.

The arboreal behavior of green iguanas has been both a blessing and a curse to the program.   An iguana likes to stake out one tree and claim it as its home and territory, where it basks and feeds, so campesinos do not have to worry about their investment scampering off deep into the forest.   Also, although iguanas grow faster if released into trees, the practice leads to a few other problems.   If the trees are too near crops—a typical scenario if the trees are used as buffers in between crops to prevent erosion— iguanas may not be able to resist feasting on the readily available buffet.   Worse yet, if the trees border a neighbor's farm, the iguanas might just eat the neighbor's profits.

Why not keep them in large pens?   Food, then, becomes an expense, as opposed to iguanas released into fruit trees, which require no feeding, since they take care of themselves by munching on treetop leaves, mangoes, and papayas at their leisure.   The tree-dwelling iguanas still leave fruit for the campesino, although for heavy stocking of trees, some supplemental feeding is required.   Caged iguanas also take longer to reach "harvesting" weight—up to five years for a 5-pound iguana that is able to feed a family of four or five.   Many campesinos concerned with making ends meet, week to week, simply cannot wait that long to spoon up that iguana stew.

The culinary climate is completely different in the central provinces, better known as "*El Interior*."   Since the campesinos of Coclé and southern Veraguas have virtually wiped iguanas out of the region, they were much more willing to participate in the project. Gonzalez nodded with satisfaction as he informed me that 100 iguana farmers from *El Interior* have been enjoying the project for years. Well-run iguana farms can yield 300 kilograms of meat per year per hectare—that's 5 to 10 times as productive as raising cattle on the same land—with the added benefit that, with a "herd" of iguanas, the erosion-fighting trees remain standing.

Some farmers utilize a mixed system, in which they still raise other livestock and grow other crops while keeping iguanas in a caged shelter, providing a diverse yield. Other farmers have even profitably sold some iguana meat to their neighbors (presently, technological and political barriers preclude the realization of large profits from iguana farming, preventing the practice from becoming more popular). Still others enjoy raising them for fun. The species itself has shared in the program's rewards as well; thus far, over 10,000 iguanas have been returned to the wilds of Panama.

As an added benefit, iguanas can also provide a reason to keep trees on one's property and help preserve the remaining tropical forests. In 1850, 92 percent of Panama was covered by forest. By 1986, the percentage had been reduced to 37 percent, almost entirely due to the voracious needs of short-term profit farming and ranching. When farmers clear a plot of tropical land using the slash and burn technique—still a common sight (and smell) in many parts of Panama—the tropical soil provides a bountiful crop for one or two years, owing to the nutrients in the burned material. Soon after, however, the plot becomes a desiccated wasteland that often requires 20 years before it is reclaimed by forest. Long before then, the farmer has moved on to another plot. If large swatches of land are cleared using this technique, the area risks becoming a desert. Since the forest is not only the habitat of the iguana, but also thousands of other plants and animals, the action of preserving tropical forest, in effect, preserves the entire ecosystem.

Of course, believing that the iguana can provide the lizardly linchpin capable of holding together the Western Hemisphere's tropical ecosystems would be naïve. After all, humans must make the choice to balance their needs and those of the environment. However, thanks to the iguana, conservation has never been so delectable.

12.
Bad Bread

"ON THIS ISLAND, THERE IS NO WATER," stated the handwritten message hanging in the bathroom of the Niskua Lodge. That didn't stop a timid, but steady stream of the elusive liquid tumbling forth when I turned the knob on the faucet, for the true meaning of the reminder was, in essence, "All potable water on this island is stored in large plastic canisters and has been collected from rain or brought in by boat. Don't be a selfish bastard by taking a half-hour shower."

Even during the rainy season on the country's Caribbean coast, a downpour is not guaranteed every afternoon, especially in September. The 370 unrelenting people of the isle of Wichub Wala have tried to run an aqueduct from the mountains on the mainland down to the island, as several of their sister islands to the east had accomplished, by simply using plastic tubing, valves, and gravity. But geography has not been kind to Wichub Wala. The islanders have found it difficult to locate a powerful enough water source originating from the particular features of the coastal mountains across the island.

From a glance, one might not have guessed that the isle's inhabitants carried on without running aqueduct water. As I navigated the walkways in between the clusters of dwellings, freshly washed clothes hung on lines; thirst of basketball players was quenched; bread was baked. For this community of Kuna, a people indigenous to the isthmus, fresh water—like the population of traditional game animals, lobsters in the reefs, and palms for thatching roofs—is just another resource they have respected enough to conserve.

I had never seen the inner workings of a Kuna bakery before. On other islands, when I did see a tiny "*Panaderia*" sign, I did not want to enter, since the *panaderias* (bakeries) always doubled as someone's private house. But when I stopped at the threshold of the *panaderia* on Wichub Wala, the couple waved me in, since a fresh batch of bread was arriving. (And fresh is when to score them, since Kuna bread is not made for shelf life: after the bread reaches ambient temperature and sits, it loses its fleeting crunch and cloudlike heart.)

Simply a windowless room of vertical cane walls atop a packed dirt floor, the bakery was anchored by its only piece of furniture: a metal range oven just like any other—it could have been ripped out of a matching kitchen set from a slummy rental apartment—except it ran on fuel from a tank. The family was busy midwifing a row of loaves the size of hot dog buns from the bottom rack. I arrived just in time to receive a handful of the scorching puffs—literally, a handful: this bakery cared not for fancy bags printed with the establishment's name (not that it had a name anyway), nor containers of any kind, and, instead, offered naked morsels hot enough to melt the cheese they sold by the slice. In an urgent rhythm, I juggled the embers out of the house while politely declining offers to purchase used clothing the family had displayed on a clothesline.

Such commerce exhibits one of the many uses of a Kuna house. In addition to the thrift shop/bakery combination above, other houses in Kuna communities double as general stores and even ice cream parlors, the latter only requiring a gas-powered refrigerator, a few wrapped up ice cream bars, and a small, hand painted "*helado*" sign.

Other families have found that their houses are busy enough just serving as homes. Without any sign of frustration, one islander informed me—and his conditions are rather typical—that he and his wife share a one-room structure with his extended family, a dog, a cat, three parrots, a chicken, and their newborn. Now that's love.

* * *

In the daytime, I found it difficult to find a pathway where a woman was not selling reverse appliqué molas, either by hanging them on the wall outside her house or by delicately holding a stitched work under her eyes like a veil. The late morning and early afternoon are prime times when long boats from hotels on nearby islands (and from cruise ships) deposit tourists looking to scarf up molas bearing the designs of their liking—anything from sea turtles and birds to whatever the mola designer wished to colorfully embalm in several layers of fabric.

Many crafts fashioned by Amerindian peoples shoved into cash economies across the Americas have been created solely for the purpose of extracting tourist dollars. Molas, however, are works that many Kuna women (and a few Kuna drag queens) have been sewing and wearing for generations. The women on Wichub Wala saved their best works for their own dresses. Even in Ipetí, a mainland Kuna community far from Kuna Yala and without any hotel or tourist facilities—subsequently, receiving few visitors outside of Peace Corps volunteers and backpackers—most of the Kuna women choose to wear dresses sewn with intense, detailed, and original molas, without one going for sale.

During a walk around the flat, almost treeless island, I noticed that while the mola trade is certainly an important player in the commerce of the island, it merely seemed to augment a permeating yet unhurried din. A basketball game swirled about on the court near the dock, the ball still defiantly managing a respectable bounce off the packed dirt. Crabs danced in and out of their holes along footpaths. Shoeless children used a crate as a step to purchase a soda through a store's sale window. A man enjoyed an al-fresco haircut while his pet parrot, uncaged and curious, attempted to nibble the fallen snippings. And then the afternoon's guerilla rainfall attacked, sending everyone indoors but, fortunately, tipping off the island's precious cache.

* * *

After a half-hour boat ride to the outlying islets to the northeast, I was introduced to the area's other active inhabitants: the population of the coral reef. One brief dunk just a foot underneath the surface transported me into a nano-metropolis where life is tangled with itself in some absurdly tight symbiotic pretzel.   Striped sergeant fish, wrasses, and yellow-blue beaugregories all darted about urchins and living sea rocks in a space no larger than a bedroom. It was like a stealthy peek into an alternate universe, yet the fidgety neon personalities and alien-brain coral can easily succumb to the pollution of the world above the waterline—a reality all the more damning since the reefs also provide us with common, if not thankless, services of combating erosion and protecting nearby land from storm surges.

When I floated and let the waves buffet me back and forth, the fish treated me as a piece of detritus around which to hide and hang out.   So many characters, so many colors, so many adaptations. I no longer wondered how a Kuna lobster diver could hold his breath for so long.

Except when they have occasionally harvested coral to enlarge their islands, the Kuna have proven worthy stewards in preserving the reefs and have even received assistance from an unlikely source: smugglers. A few decades ago, in the anonymous darkness of night, a Colombian ship misjudged the water depth around the archipelago and ran aground about 50 feet from nearby Isla Perro, the crew abandoning the hopelessly stuck vessel. While the memories of the residents I spoke with cannot agree on what type of contraband the boat had been carrying or what year the boat made its last fateful run, the smuggler's loss was clearly the reef's gain. The coral and the fish instantly became smitten with the new protruding chunk of submarine topography and moved right in. In some areas of the sunken hull, colonies of coral have grown so thick that the curvature of the boat is obscured. As rust has bored larger openings into the hull, more critters have made the contraband condo their home. Squatters keepers.

Just in case any smugglers pass by the same route nowadays, they'll be immediately notified of the previous failure, since part of the wreck still protrudes above the waterline, even during high tide.

* * *

As night relieves day back at Wichub Wala, the mola displays disappear, supplanted by the meditative lambency of kerosene lamps and wood fires escaping from the gaps in the houses' cane reed walls. Trebly radios pick up scatterings of reception from the mainland. Across from the Niskua Lodge, the lamp from inside the grocery store Centro Kike (pronounced KEE-KAY, a Spanish nickname for Enrique and not related to anything anti-Semitic), doubles as the only streetlight, the lodge's solar panels resting for the night.

I wondered what endeavors the islanders reserved for nightlife. Regulations on recreational pastimes such as billiards and booze can vary acutely from island to island. Would there be a place to grab a beer and enjoy the breezes of the evening? One night I walked to the Centro Kike window to find the young clerk loading a battery-operated cassette deck.

"There are no bars here," Patrick, the clerk, nodded with a condoling slowness.

"It's prohibited," added Gomez, owner of the other pair of elbows on the service window shelf. His bony shoulders protruded from a basketball jersey for the island's team. Their wives, gracefully bound in beaded wrist and ankle bracelets, reclined in the corners of the amber-flashed interior.

Patrick gestured around his store and said, "Well, we don't have a billiards table inside the store, but we have beer and music. And chairs. And conversation. Would you like to come in?" And, thus, I had found a place to grab a beer and enjoy the breezes of the evening.

Centro Kike is one of the island's three standalone grocery stores, each concrete structure funded by a different political party and named after its patron. The bulky structure provided plenty of room inside—in fact, enough space for a forbidden pool table— but instead, stocked little more than a cooler, a few boxes of detergent, and a collection of single-use bags of cooking oil. Cuts from a Colombian pop diva, arriving next on Patrick's playlist, filled the rest of the store. "Do you like Colombian music?" Patrick asked. "We are very familiar with Colombian music, since the Colombian trading vessels stop by frequently. More frequently than Panamanian vessels. We see many American boats here too. Because of them, our Spanish has become a little different than that of the mainland. For *azúcar*, we say '*soo*-gar.' Smoother, no?" He pointed at the change received for my beer. "For *dinero*, we say 'money.'"

American English was not the only linguistic import exhibited in the store. After years on a globe-combing freighter vessel, Gomez returned to Kuna Yala with smatterings of Greek and Japanese language skills. The crewman began to illustrate knowledge of the fledgling Japanese wine industry I hadn't found anywhere else—not even from a wine shop I had visited while I was in Tokyo some years back. Who knew that to learn about the grape varieties grown in southern Japan, I would have to go to Panama?

With a foray of foreign transfusions, what about bonds across the San Blás Mountain Range to the rest of Panama? 80 years had passed since Kuna Yala revolted against Panamanian colonialism and won autonomy. A new president, Martín Torrijos, son of a Panamanian dictator from decades past, had just been inaugurated a few days before. Might the new administration offer new opportunities for the autonomous province? "He already forgot about us," the men shot back. They said that Torrijos' campaign schedule had mostly omitted Kuna Yala. (The sponsor of Centro Kike belonged to a political party different from that of the new president.) Political differences didn't seem to stop Patrick from enjoying salsa, a national institution of Panama. After a little goading, he demonstrated his steps on the concrete floor—as smooth as *soo*-gar, I must say.

As the clerk/bartender/deejay switched to an old, muffled tape of Abba, conversation turned to island news. A new building was being constructed. As with most other Kuna communities when a family needs to build a new house, the village meets in their congress hall and chips in with financial assistance and, more importantly, labor—for instance, boating to the mainland and harvesting *ueruk* palm leaves for the roof and white cane for the walls.

"On the island we are all equal," Gomez added. And, in fact, the island already tendered an answer to the unbalancing effects of the cash economy's gradual creep. The new construction in question was not for a family—it would, eventually, house a business exclusively and, unlike with family dwellings, the island community is not obliged to help out in the construction of a business. The island's rock-hemmed lobster pool, too, is a business. Even the lodge had to purchase lobsters from the pool's manager. But no one else had to help in the laborious task of constructing the pool's stone barriers. The system seems to pit community ties against capital accumulation but, since the Kuna alone control the economy of their province, they alone control the outcome. What's next for the island? Picket fences? Somehow, I doubt it, although electricity has already been run from the mainland to supply a lone house complete with a couch and a television (I would guess, however, that no one had to help carry that couch from the dock).

Alas, the salsa had sipped the last life from the batteries. Patrick and Gomez were preparing to close up the shop. I finished my beer and thanked the clerks for their hospitality. "See you tomorrow morning," I said.

"*Panemalo*," Patrick responded. What could *panemalo* mean? It sounded as if he had uttered a bouncy rendition of *pan mal*, or Spanish for "bad bread." He must have been warning me that the bread would be old and stale tomorrow morning. Now that he had broached the issue, I had recalled that the bread served for breakfast at the lodge could not compete with the blister-worthy offering straight from the baker that I had juggled earlier in the day. But who am I to judge an island with such drive as to surmount a lack of running water? How could I fault a community whose lodge for outsiders lies in the middle of its snugly arranged buildings, permitting the visitor a capillary-side view of the island's pumping life? The only appropriate response, I thought, was to thank Patrick for such honest advice.

"*Gracias* — "

"*Panemalo* means 'see you later' in Kuna," he said.

Needless to say, I was glad he did not give me a chance to finish the thought. The lodge's honor has been defended.

But I now have an unforgettable mnemonic for the translation.

13.

How Not to Watch Turtles

WHEN A TOWN IS GIVEN FREEDOM to choose its own nickname, one might expect it to favor a romantic caricature. Maybe a cute, fudgy epithet. But the southern town of Tonosí instead capitalized on the opportunity to make a statement. The sign marking the entry of the ranching town nakedly declares TONOSÍ, THE FORGOTTEN VILLAGE.

Who forgot Tonosí? "The government," my cabbie answered through creased lips, while he swerved to avoid another gouge in the road the size of a bass drum. At least this time, he didn't need to delicately skirt the side of the road to evade the crevice. All three roads leading to Tonosí suffer from a gruesome case of pothole acne, a jolting switch from the well-tarred, main artery running from the capital to the border of Costa Rica.

Aside from the occasional surfer pursuing monster waves rolling into the Pacific beaches to the south, tourists and other visitors have also forgotten Tonosí. The southern province of Los Santos, into which is carved the valley of Tonosí, is one of the least visited corners of Panama. Its hotels barely mustered up a 7 percent occupancy rate in 2002. Indeed, I was the only guest at the Tonosí hotel—the only person to enjoy a $15-per-night room with a functioning air conditioner. The dearth of visitors seemed all the more remarkable since I arrived the last day of August, a prime occasion for sea turtle nestings on the beach of Isla Caña, an island a short drive from Tonosí. A full moon would be illuminating the night sky in a few hours — facilitating easy turtle viewing.

The day before, I followed the standard Isla Caña booking protocol: call the island's only payphone, and whichever turtle guide sprints to the phone first would become yours for the evening. That night, the wingtips of a whispery man named Edgar scored him the job. I looked forward to benefiting from his 23 years on the island, maximizing my chances to find turtles under the diligent glow of the moon. Were many turtles arriving this month? "Oh yes, we saw 20 last night. One night last week, 50 came up to the beach to lay their eggs." What are the best hours to see them? "Nine to midnight," he answered, oddly coinciding with the suggestion I had made to him that I might plan for a cab back to Tonosí at midnight (how convenient!).

Pity that my careful planning did not avoid — as based on the title of this adventure — an ending of prodigious disaster. But before I flesh out the lapse of good tidings, let me explain why I sought to observe this marvelous flipper-propelled creature known as the olive ridley sea turtle. Isla Caña is the very beach at which the arriving females, themselves, had hatched years before and, after having traveled over thousands of kilometers to and from foraging grounds, the adept mariners employed their natural compasses to relocate the same tiny, 10-kilometer target — Isla Caña's beach — to start the cycle anew.

Isla Caña is only one of a handful of beaches where the olive ridleys still nest in abundance. Their worldwide number has been sinking over the past decades in an inverse proportion to human exploitation of the seas and beaches. Biologists have estimated that 20,000 female olive ridley sea turtles currently deem the beach on Isla Caña as a place suitable enough to bury their eggs in the sand.

What is suitable to an olive ridley? The beach must be sized and sloped properly, lest the eggs wash away in high tide. Any beach she has chosen in the past that has since succumbed to human development usually becomes tainted enough so that the mother will turn up her beak and leave without dropping any eggs.

Artificial light, however, is the most nefarious deterrent. Those few mothers who don't mind a little basking under streetlamps or backyard floodlights will jeopardize the future of themselves and their hatchlings, since the light confuses the turtles' reading of ambient luminescence, leading some new hatchlings to run the wrong way out of the nest and into streets where tires of trucks and jaws of predators dispense with the fledglings. The mothers, as well as the young, can die from the heat if they cannot find their way back to the ocean by the afternoon. Isla Caña's beach remains virgin, save an unlit tower built by ANAM, Panama's government-run nature management association.

The female olive ridleys are choosy and virtually faithful when it comes to beach selection but, when seeking a mate, they swing more than the tide. They indulge a different fancy every year at mating time, sometimes racking up several partners in the same season (but don't feel sorry for the males; both genders possess a flair for the wandering eye). And they like to play rough, too. Nesting mothers have been seen arriving on the beach with bite wounds on their heads, necks, and flippers, testament to the olive ridley's idea of a fun date. A female may also be nursing shell damage from savage jabs of the male's flipper claw, which he uses to hold her in place, in case she has second thoughts. If olive ridleys could write, they'd be masters of the trashy novel.

Sadly, her mating bruises may be in vain. Predators such as cats, dogs, ants, and lizards enjoy digging up the eggs for a rich meal, and the flavor of the creamy turtle eggs has not gone unnoticed by their most detrimental predator: the people of Central America, for whom the buried treasures provide a seasonal snack, often viewed as an aphrodisiac. Even if left alone by humans, only about 5 percent of the hatchlings survive the six-week incubation and reach the open sea. In Panama, as in other Central American countries, unregulated removal of turtle eggs from nesting sites is illegal, which is why island volunteers patrol the beach every nesting night with the help of armed police.

Ten kilometers of dark beach presented a challenge for two policemen to cover. I was happy to assist the local economy and ecology by patrolling the beach with the islanders, but I almost missed the last boat of the evening heading down the shallow river to Isla Caña, owing to the careful navigation of the crater slalom course leading out of Tonosí. "Please, don't forget me," I told the cabbie, after I arranged for him to pick me up at midnight at the boat launch for the return trip to Tonosí.

At the island's port, Edgar trailed behind the flickering giggles of his three restless children—his welcoming party—until they docked under Edgar's arms. He sat me down at the island's simple, open-walled restaurant, where I found the cook tucked into a corner table, his face squished into his hands. The portly cook, Fernando, dragged up his eyebrows in a brief but spiritless acknowledgement as we were introduced. Fernando was also a turtle guide, but since he lost the race to the public phone, he would only cook for the evening. Despite his defeat on the paths of the island, his form in the kitchen proved flawless, offering lightly fried plantains and a grilled, juicy snapper, the spine of which I had found myself obsessively picking clean. If his guide skills matched his culinary talent, I bet he'd predict the landfall location of each turtle within a meter.

But victory belonged to Edgar, who spoke with the unflappability of a grade school art teacher. He celebrated by ushering me around the sparse but cozy town, since stewarding the island's transient turtle population is but one source of pride for the island.   Edgar made sure to point out the island's still-functioning, manually-operated wooden *trapiches*, or cane-grinders, like the ones utilized only for display purposes in Panama City restaurants.   The island's 700 inhabitants still cultivate sugar cane, the island's namesake—for Isla Caña means "Cane Island."

Electricity and water are wired and piped, respectively, from the mainland.   Unlike the mainland, however, Isla Caña has no bad roads, since it has no roads—unless you count machete-manicured paths for foot travel and horse-drawn carts.   On the way to sign paperwork, necessary to enter the beach (a national park), Edgar pointed out the island's public phone, its antenna peeking above the treetops.   He spoke smugly, treating the wireless structure as a prized landmark.   And why not?   This piece of technology allowed him to make a little money tonight.

The vigil began after sundown.   Edgar led me to his horse to take me, in a flat cart, across the mild crescent of beach, then a nursery for thousands of incubating turtles buried beneath the surface.   Flags marked the location of the known egg deposits.   Our patrol acquired Ricardo, son of a past Panamanian diplomat, and his girlfriend, who were staying in one of the island's cabanas and were also on the hunt for nesting turtles.   "We'll be patrolling the center part of the beach," Edgar stated.   "It's too big to walk up and down the whole length."   The entire 10-kilometer beach, however, failed to intimidate the lone volunteer on duty, a woman of the island, who would, indeed, be shuffling about the entire length, sweeping back and forth all night to keep drooling poachers from the hoard of about 100 eggs from each arriving turtle.

Since steady, bright lights might confuse and scare the arriving reptilian mothers back into the ocean, we all strolled in complete darkness, save the orange glow of the moon, rising majestically, casting its fiery image onto the Pacific. Soon blips of flashlights from the eastern end of the beach pricked the ink of the night. What could the signals mean?

"That's the volunteer," Edgar pointed out. Could it be a turtle? "It could very well be a turtle," Edgar stated, "but I think it's too far. We might not make it over there in time, since a female turtle will normally finish up her egg laying in an hour. If the turtle was almost done laying eggs when the volunteer found her, then there is even less time to see her."

After seasons of patrolling the beach for nestings, I would imagine the islanders would have figured out a simple system of blinks to indicate what is going on. One blink for a turtle arriving, two for a turtle laying eggs, three for departing. After all, the world was able to successfully communicate declarations of war and winners of elections with the Morse code for an entire era. Couldn't a few turtle stewards muster up a simple visual language?

In the absence of a defined code, the anxious blinking across the beach could have signified any number of thoughts besides "I found a turtle." Perhaps "I didn't find a turtle." Or: did you find a turtle? Someone is stealing eggs and I'm out of bullets. I'm bored and feel like playing with my flashlight. I accidentally hit the switch — please disregard.

To add to the rich variation in communicative possibilities, Ricardo's girlfriend fancied the rising moon and took a photo of it. By accident, the camera's flash went off. The flash must have appeared, from afar, as a blink of a flashlight, since from the other end of the beach, the volunteer who found the turtle/did not find the turtle/asked if we found a turtle immediately answered with a blast of restless flashes, indicating "have you not received my previous messages?" Or perhaps she was telling us "send help: Panama is being invaded by a highly trained Norwegian flotilla!"

There was nothing more to do than wait. In the middle of the beach, we met the policemen on duty for the 12-hour night shift who, instead of patrolling with the volunteer, were sitting on a piece of driftwood in front of the ANAM tower chatting quietly, but amply. One of them kept busy by aiming a flashlight on his boots to ensure no biting insects were stealthily making their way up his legs.

Talking won't scare the turtles? "Don't worry, we're not talking loud enough for that," Edgar responded. "We have been trained by biologists." The moon edged higher and brighter as we departed the driftwood post and headed a little west, further away from the volunteer, who, by then, no doubt, had been taken hostage by sniggering Nordic soldiers who forced her to eat lutefisk.

Waylaying more time, we continued to amble westward. "I feel good about being a guide," beamed Edgar, who moved to Isla Caña 23 years ago and views protecting turtles as a pleasure and a duty. He enjoys living on the island – there is no traffic or crime. The only recent development arrived in the form of a few cabanas for tourists. Many food items are grown on or fished from the island. As we shuffled through the sand, his island tales recounted retired Americans who saw the island just once, fell in love with it, and wanted to spend the rest of their days husking coconuts and harvesting watermelons. And patiently waiting for turtles to nest.

After an hour, we turned around and began walking eastward, past the driftwood cops diligently keeping bugs off their pants, until we met the out-of-breath volunteer. "Two turtles were nesting," she said in between puffs of air. "They just started to dig the holes when I got there. I signaled. Why didn't you come?"

Edgar explained how far away we were. I figured I could have covered the 3 or 4 kilometers or so in about 40 minutes, faster if I walked like the New Yorker I am. But there was little sense in fretting over a missed chance, I thought. If 50 turtles, a typical number for this time of year, arrived in the next two hours, that's 25 an hour or, roughly, one turtle every 400 meters, on average.

But olive ridleys do not care much for averages. The olive ridleys, as a defense against predators, normally synchronize their beach arrivals in movements known as *arribadas,* to inundate the beach with eggs, leaving too many treats for all the predators to gourmandize in one sitting. The strategy also ensures that the eggs will hatch at the same time, providing a beach full of baby turtles scampering towards the water, increasing chances that birds and crabs in the area will feast on a few turtles and then reach their fill, allowing the rest of the hatchlings to reach the ocean.

The two turtles to the east were most likely loners, which meant that the massive *arribada* had yet to arrive. Each olive ridley female is about 2 feet long. Her flippers awkwardly scurry up the beach, leaving a gouged-out path in the sand under her 70-pound weight. You can't miss 'em.

Only ghost crabs, translucent and fleeting on their tiptoes, roamed the beach with us. The crabs, the fastest crustaceans on land, were undoubtedly waiting for the baby turtles to hatch, since the tiny, blundering flippers of a hatchling offer no match for the crabs' seasoned agility when the crab drags the hatchling into its beach hole. Fresh turtle take-out.

The inquisitive crabs, their black eyes quivering, would have to wait for the baby turtles to depart from the top of the beach, just as we would have to wait for the mothers to arrive from sea. More moonlight chatter ensued, touching upon snakes, insects, politics — everything but turtles, as if not to jinx us.

The volunteer had already trudged down towards the western end of the beach and began to blink her flashlight with urgent excess. But we had already headed east, and Edgar recommended that we continue eastward.

Ricardo and company had been shown Edgar's latest project: a building for visitors just 50 meters from the beach. The structure had no electricity (lights might deter turtles from arriving) and no walls. But with a dousing of DEET spray, the couple chose to leave the cabana on the other end of the island and stay under the roof cradled by the nocturnal chorus of unseen tropical insects and animals. "If you need to, you can stay here too," Ricardo told me.

"Thanks for the offer. I just might have to stay here if the cabbie doesn't arrive at the port."

Midnight had begun its approach. "Two were nesting in the western part of the beach. I signaled," the volunteer blurted when she met us at the middle driftwood. Such strafes of tantalizing misfortune seemed like taunts from the ocean, taunts from a curious mustering of reptilian wit. I began to think I should have allowed more time, but since I had no way of contacting the cabbie, I did not want to be remembered as the irresponsible *pendejo* who made him wait at the port for nothing. I imagined he probably had a few cold beers waiting for him at a bar as soon as he dropped me off.

Meanwhile, the minutes mercilessly ticked, and I knew I still had to cross over to the mainland. To take me to the port, Edgar fetched the horse, its head bobbing in protest on each step, for the beast could not be convinced to gallop any faster than the pace of a walking person. But I could not have simply bolted across the island, since I needed Edgar to wake up the boatman. As I remembered it, the river trip only lasted about three minutes in an outboard motorboat. Would the cab driver decide to flee the port and hit the bars if I were very late?

When we arrived at the island's boat launch, everything looked different: a geographical shell game. The launch area had grown much larger and muddier. Where did that river go? And then the weight of reality struck me with porno mag subtlety: I was staring at the channel at low tide. Yes, I had forgotten to check the tide tables. The kilometer journey up the mainland river, en route to the port, had drained, leaving a trough of mischievous sludge.

"It will be easier if you take your shoes off," Edgar commented.

The boatman arrived to float me across the tiny, token snippet of water remaining in the channel and, after abandoning the boat, he beckoned me to lower my feet into the black, slimy ravine that six hours before provided a water-filled, three-minute motorized breeze through the mangrove swamp. I followed him as his calves disappeared into the riverbed with each step, and discovered that there was no efficient way to scramble through the mud groping at my feet. One step at a time was the limit. One barefoot in, one barefoot out. I failed to find comfort in the fact that skin care addicts pay $300 to have this kind of clammy silt spread over them at spas. Did I need cucumber slices over my eyes—and a trickle of ambient world music—to properly activate the mud's charm?

Since the riverbed followed a naturally wavy path upstream, and the swarm of trees surrounding the gully denied us the benefit of the full moon's beam, I could not spot the mainland boat launch to see whether the cab had already fled. If he had, then I knew I would have to administer another spa treatment to myself by heading all the way back to the island for the night. In the dour absence of light, the crooning of crickets and swooping insects added their heckling commentary.

It was half-past 12 when we arrived at the port, that stumpy lip of earth, lit by the headlights of a pickup truck, a comfortingly familiar truck: my taxi. I washed off my legs (now exfoliated by exotic minerals, I reckon) under the port's only adornment: a spigot.

Tangled up in a snoring tranquility, the cabbie, Leonardo, had sprawled himself out in the cab of the pickup truck, gaunt limbs sprouting like overgrown sugar cane. He had neatly balanced his straw *sombrero pintado* — literally, a "painted hat" owing to its weaved-in ring of dyed black reeds — over his face.

Navigating the gouges in Tonosí's roads at 1 a.m. brought Leonardo back to full alertness as he clutched the steering wheel possessively with both hands, his face crumpled in concentration. His larynx, however, operated loosely and contentedly. "Did you see any turtles?"

After recounting the evening, I figured I'd earned myself a beer or two as well. Leonardo informed me, however, that no bars in town remained open. So he took me back to the empty hotel.

But the hotel was no longer empty. As I switched on the light, I noticed that a fleet of dexterous cockroaches had decided to bunk with me. These didn't represent a Central American jungle variety; rather, they were the standard breed-o-matics, the adept hitchhikers normally found scrambling through the cracks of your favorite city.

I didn't relish the idea of spending the whole night in pursuit of winged critters that have actually developed separate, simplified brains that control their hind legs to facilitate quicker reactions, whilst I stubbed my toes on the concrete bed frame, ad nauseam. Besides, the last time I had heard of concrete bed frames was when reviewing the history of Pompeii, where the brothels had employed concrete because wood frames kept breaking when the women fulfilled their clients' desired tasks. Maybe I was not in a hotel at all. It was time to leave.

Since the office was closed and the hotel remained empty and coal dark, I left a brief note as to why I would be wandering the sedate roads of Tonosí in search of another place to sleep. Lonely Planet's guidebook of Panama, already 4 years old (but, nonetheless, the most recent guidebook available at the time), listed another hotel's address by use of street names and directions. But Tonosí, like most of Central America, regards street signs as crutches for wimps. The directions from the book, therefore, were useless. The book sported many maps of other towns and cities around Panama on which I had depended innumerable times before, but it omitted any cartographical representation of Tonosí, the Forgotten Village.

Instead of observing the magic of the olive ridley renewing its fragile life cycle, I was roaming the stagnant shadows of a southern Panamanian farming town in the early morning, kicking up dead soil that was drier than a discount wedding cake. Everyone in town was asleep, of course, to prepare for the next day of farm work.

Fortunately, Tonosí only claims so many streets, so after half an hour of wandering under the weight of my duffel bag, I found the mystical second hotel.   The office, as expected, was empty. What to do? I shouted as lightly as I could. "*¿Hola?*"

Sleeping under the hotel's overhang looked agreeable, since the kitchen, complete with refrigerator, stood outside, all within easy access. Maybe if I just quietly take a bottle and leave small change in its place—

A mustached man barely wrapped in a white towel appeared from the door off the kitchen.

"I'm really sorry to wake you. Do you have a room available? Again, I'm sorry—"

"No need to apologize," the toweled man answered, with carefully narrowed eyes. "What kind of room do you want?"

His question required the usual answer: single, double, private bath, air conditioner, telephone—but apparently the journey through the clam-juice air had disturbingly altered my standards, for I heard myself answering with "A room with a bed, and no roaches."

His squinting intensified. Without responding, he walked me up the stairs and showed me a pink room with cracked ceiling tiles but, otherwise, simple and clean. And, thus, I spent the night in Tonosí, completely free of roaches. And, alas, completely free of turtles.

* * *

As the sun charged the next morning, trucks and vans chugged by, slathered with TONOSÍ, THE FORGOTTEN VILLAGE bumper stickers. I ate the hotel's last tortilla, a puck of sweet corn rather than an enchilada-esque wrap, along with a red *salchicha*, a sausage popular in Los Santos.

The restaurant, at ground level and below the rooms, was open on three sides, a fact over which I labored. I would be in clear view if the first hotel's owner, perturbed by my sudden departure, came looking for me. Neither hotel asked for identification or a signature, but I was probably the only out-of-towner afoot. I'd be a snap to recognize in this small town. And the next bus running further north wasn't scheduled for another two hours. Would they call the police on the misbehaving gringo over a $15 room? Aw, that's silly.

As my mind began to generously foment such unsavory scenarios, a pickup truck with government markings pulled up to the restaurant. Two policemen squared their shiny boots onto the pavement and began swaggering towards me.

Do they serve *salchichas* in Panamanian prison?

I doubt it, because I've never heard a good thing about Panamanian incarceration. The notoriously crowded conditions have forced many accused to sleep on the floor of cells during their pre-trial detention periods lasting indefinitely. Prisoners have been known to get beheaded here and there.

As the policemen stepped closer, I recognized them as the guards from the 12-hour night shift on Isla Caña's beach. They had arrived at the restaurant to eat. They only thing on which they could bust me was eating the last tortilla.

"Any bugs make it up your pant legs?" I wanted to inquire. Instead, I asked how the rest of the night passed.

"Lots of turtles—20, maybe 30 arrived together at about 4 in the morning."

Perhaps I had misunderstood Edgar when we discussed the best time to view the nestings. In any case, at that moment I wished that the cabbie from the Forgotten Village had forgotten to meet me at the port the night before.

14.

Ipetí

FROM WITHIN THE CONCRETE TAPESTRY of Panama City, urbanites informed me that a cockfight of cultures could be rubbernecked three hours east of the capital. They were referring to the 30-year-old town of Ipetí, where an indigenous Kuna community sits across the highway from a village of the Kuna's historical neighbors, the Emberá. While such proximate diversity may seem expected in a country in which 10 percent of its population remains indigenous, the coziness of the town raises interest for the simple fact that the Kuna and Emberá are also historical archenemies, the two neighbors claiming centuries of skirmishes in what is now eastern Panama and western Colombia.

But that was the past. Surely the neighbors had made amends by now? In response, a fountain of words flew a bit too easily from the smirks of *capitaleños*.

"The word for enemy in the Kuna language is 'Emberá.'"

"They don't talk to each other on the bus and, once they get off, they stay on their own sides of the highway."

"They hate each other."

Indeed, based on their description of the current relationship of the two peoples, I should duck to avoid a war of projectiles when the public bus passes through Ipetí. I wasn't planning on passing through Ipetí, however. I was going to stop there.

A flip of a Balboa *centavo* (coinage is the only Panamanian-minted currency and is equivalent to its U.S. counterpart) dictated which side of the highway at Ipetí I would explore first: the bust of Urraca, a chief who revolted against Spanish conquest, stared back at me from the head of the coin, thus I selected the northern side, host to the Kuna's thatched roof houses and dirt floors.

Not that either side boasted regular accommodation of any ilk. To the south, the Emberá's plan to build cabanas had reached little beyond the grand but fantastical oral phase. On the Kuna side, I was offered crash space in a roadside tool shed on the floor next to bags of concrete and a few bunches of plantains that didn't sell that day. Alezio, the young clerk of Ipetí Kuna's general store, offered the lodging and, in exchange, I bought him needed bicycle parts, as well as meals at a rustic Panamanian restaurant of which Alezio was rather fond. The eatery lay just up the highway in Ipetí's third community, Ipetí Colono, consisting of a few hundred *mestizos*, also referred to as *colonos*, who moved to the region from the central provinces to raise cattle.

Clad in a t-shirt and cutoff shorts that wouldn't find themselves out of place at an American punk rock show, Alezio sold highway travelers everything from sugar to cigarettes to tampons. At night, he slept in a hammock at the back of the zinc-roofed store.

Reminiscent of other Kuna communities, the tiny din of mola-clad Kuna women gabbing amongst themselves burbled in the air. Kids, demonstrating a liberal view of what clothing is really necessary, swarmed around me and requested that I take their photos again and again (they figured out the instant gratification of my digital camera's view screen rather swiftly). Close to their basketball court, their long *chicha* house awaited the next festivity — probably a Kuna puberty ceremony, an event celebrating a girl's arrival to womanhood—where the entire village sips gourds filled with *inna*, a brew fermented from sugar cane and corn (and plantains, in this village's case), stored for up to two weeks in underground jugs to attain its classic strength.

Ipetí Kuna is not part of the better-known, Atlantic-side province of Kuna Yala, where the Kuna revolted against Panama's restrictions of Kuna culture in 1925 and gained a substantial degree of autonomy. Owing to separate migrations of Kuna and occasional infighting among Kuna groups, some Kuna communities settled inland instead of on the coast. Ipetí Kuna, one of the inland communities, lies just inside the border of Madungandi, a separate Kuna-administered comarca formed out of the central Panama province in 1996. The comarca does not claim the same level of autonomy as Kuna Yala and, only recently, received titles for its land. Unlike the practically virgin mountain slopes of its brethren's comarca to the north, large areas of the jungles of central Panama have already been shorn clean, making it difficult for the people of Madungandi to live off the land as in the past, hence a new reliance on cash.

Unlike the tourist-accustomed Kuna islands of the Caribbean, where the Kuna women serve as colorful and "exotic" subjects for many a tourist's viewfinder, Ipetí had not yet bothered levying a charge for taking photos of its people. Then again, also unlike the islands, no idyllic crystal seawater laps up against the community, since Ipetí is landlocked. Faded plastic wrappers dot the packed dirt walkways. Flush toilets remain a fantasy; open holes in the ground, artifacts of outhouses of years past, are marked with nothing but their unsavory darkness within, awaiting a careless step. The new privy also consists of just a hole except it has been fortified with walls and, curiously, a lock on the *outside* (and trust me, there is nothing to steal on the inside). The women sew the vivid, intricate molas to beautify their own clothing, as opposed to the women of the islands who also hawk them to cruise ship passengers. Aside from highway travelers in need of a bunch of plantains or a pack of smokes, only the Peace Corps and the occasional backpacker tend to visit Ipetí Kuna.

Like Kuna Yala, Ipeti Kuna claims a history of interference by the government. Ipeti was created 30 years ago as a place to shuffle indigenous villages away from what would become the bed of the now-dammed Lake Bayano. Since both Kuna and Emberá communities had been utilizing the fertile land that was to be flooded, albeit far from one another, the relocation placed them across the road from each other.

Our tongues slickened by the restaurant's sole selection, *pollo frito,* or fried chicken, Alezio and I enjoyed a pleasant lunch in a town with an otherwise unpleasant past of forced relocation and inter-tribal strife. So where was the low intensity war zone spoke of so flippantly in the city? Ah, but we were having lunch in the *colono* third of the town—neutral ground, to be sure.

Perhaps, I thought, I would find the front line near a resource over which control has historically been a source of battles across the globe: water. An aqueduct on the Emberá side, completed by the government two years ago, provides potable water for both sides of the highway (except for Ipetí Colono, which is separated from the other two communities by a river; the town possesses its own water source). Sharing is essential and provides an alternative to using water from the Ipetí River that flows by the Emberá and then the Kuna, but has already been contaminated with agricultural runoff and browned with sediment from deforestation.

The aqueduct provides an alternative, when it's working, that is. Since its tube tapped an unluckily weak mountain source, one day the aqueduct would yield water, the next nothing, and the government had not gotten around to fixing the miscalculation. Merrily, the day I arrived, the spigots ran wet.

I was already looking forward to a mountain-cold shower the next morning, under the sun in the stall behind Alezio's store but, first, could I see the aqueduct? Alezio volunteered himself as a guide to the other side of the highway—deep in enemy territory, nonetheless. Unlike Ipetí Kuna, which abutted the highway, Ipetí Emberá ensconced itself a mile south of the highway (a demilitarized zone?). We would approach the aqueduct by means of Alezio's two bicycles. I should have gone supply shopping with Alezio beforehand, for I was assigned the bicycle with no brakes. Alezio's vehicle fared worse; his chain snapped during the trip. So we ended up with one bike that couldn't start and another that couldn't stop.

Emberá families underneath roofs of pole houses met their enemy by waving at him and his American observer. Fenceless chickens pecked up all they desired. Soccer teams continued parrying around oblivious foraging roosters. A hike up to the squat concrete aqueduct tank drew little more than a therapeutic view of Ipetí Emberá's rich and still-existent tropical forest. Had we visited the correct village?

As we returned to Ipetí Kuna's roadside fruit stand, each of us encumbered by crippled machinery, a figure relaxing against the railing nodded to us with siesta-hour docility, the man's gaunt chest emblazoned with an Ipetí Emberá basketball shirt. He was chatting in Spanish to a few Kuna men behind rows of plantain bunches. Had there been a truce?

After holding up my end of the lodging agreement by purchasing bicycle chains and brakes at the general store in Ipetí Colono, we returned to the restaurant for dinner. The television in front of its adjoining grocery store had become a theater, the lot radiating with an attentive crescent of seated admirers from each of the three Ipetí communities. Such harmony! But why? Had the television, that universal tractor beam of electromagnetic heroin, preempted the war?

I decided to fuel up at the restaurant before I considered the situation further. The waitress, the same from lunchtime, offered us *pollo frito* again. Was there anything else? "I have pork," she answered while tilting her head to soften the expected qualification, "but it's *very* greasy." A slow spin of the hand on her belly and a clown's grimace provided punctuation. Alezio did not mind the gastronomic repetition and went for his beloved *pollo frito* and, since I was curious to experience for myself my host's average daily routine, I took the waitress' advice and opted for what seemed to be the lesser of two greases anyway. It would be *pollo frito* for me again.

While Alezio seemed soundly content working the joints of the fried chicken, others from the comarca had long since moved away for work in the capital, the Canal, or ocean-streaming merchant vessels. The population of Ipetí Kuna thus lists heavily toward the young: 50 percent of the village's population is under 15 years of age. "Would you ever consider moving to the city?" I asked.

"There's a lot of crime there," he replied. And here, in the boonies, only the criminals of scatological partiality seem to present a problem.

Alezio had lived here all his life. He was an ideal subject to ask for a clarification on current indigenous politics. "So is it true," I asked Alezio in between gnaws, "that the word for enemy in the Kuna language is 'Emberá'?"

Before I describe his reply, I must say that I have never seen anyone unceremoniously approach a piece of fried chicken like Alezio, who must flatter the cook every time he leaves bones on the plate in scorching time. After I placed my question, however, his oral machinery shut down in abnormal seizure, and he tweaked his face as if I had asked him if he had been to Jupiter recently.

"No. It's a different word." He then proceeded to dispense with the rest of his *pollo frito* without missing a bite.

* * *

What would be an introduction to the town without a sampling of its nightlife? For that, Alezio walked me eight steps from the restaurant's dining area to the back room, revealing Ipetí's only pool table. A dull patina of dust blown off nearby crops stuck to everything, even though I arrived in August—the middle of rainy season—a telling sign of the breadth of cleared areas in what used to be a virgin tropical forest 30 years before.

A cue stick's length away from the table, the fully functional latrine trough paired itself with a fully nonfunctional sink whose rings of sediment begged for archaeological investigation. The only other two patrons tenderly stewed themselves in cigarette smoke and a growth of empty beer bottles. Turquoise walls, well gouged wherever they have scuffled with furniture, trapped the loafing smell of piss and fertilizer. A sign at the bar read WE HAVE CEVICHE.

Fifty-cent beers lubricated my losing streak, until the shimmering crucifix of Alezio's bracelet dragged across the felt to award me one last defeat. We walked back across the bridge to Ipetí Kuna, where I retired to the slab walls of the shed, taking care not to trip over the stash of plantains and half-working bicycles.

It was then that I discovered a disadvantage of the more expensive and prestigious slab houses versus the traditional Kuna houses of vertical cane reed walls (in Ipetí's case, thin branches have been substituted), the latter style slowly—and sadly—being supplanted by the former. Sound enters and passes through the gaps between the reeds of a Kuna house's walls — perhaps a prima facie disadvantage. But the slab houses — built from flat, inch-thick boards of squared off tropical hardwood and topped with a thin zinc roof — fence in the incoming sound and reverberate it, such that reclining inside a slab house is akin to shoving one's head into a drum. And nature is the spasmodic percussionist. Every lizard, raspy-legged insect, or other nocturnal creature that so much as crawled a few steps upon a wall or roof of the shed roared with the clamor of a whole cabal of them dancing around me. Roosters whose internal clocks seemed to have been set to the rise of the moon instead of the sun screeched in quadraphonic ecstasy.

In the morning, while the branch-walled houses heated up gracefully and allowed breezes to pass through, the slabs and the metal roof of the shed created an insulated oven that baked me right out of bed. No worries, however. I walked over to the roofless outdoor shower stall for a splashing of cold mountain water. I turned the valve atop the plastic pipe, closed my eyes, and felt absolutely *dry*. "Welcome to Ipetí," said the valve.

I found Alezio's greased fingers fiddling with a bike chain underneath the overhang of his store. Was there a problem with the water pressure this morning? He bent down and twisted a few knobs poking from half-buried pipes that led under the highway to the aqueduct. "No water today," he replied with formulaic indifference normally reserved for such statements as "No mail today." (But you wouldn't hear the latter anyway, since Ipetí Kuna doesn't have a post office.)

That hapless logistic did not stop the Kuna and Emberá alike from bathing in the Ipetí River, as they braved the agricultural runoff and whatever else that made several of them sick from previously drinking it. Then again, where else could they have bathed?

Alezio didn't seem to mind my aura of sweat as he requested that we walk across the bridge to his favorite restaurant for breakfast.   The same waitress brought us the morning's only offering—*pollo frito*, of course.

* * *

In lieu of a feud between tribes, the villages had, instead, been fighting as allies in the battle for potable water. Besides the villagers' own daily requirements, another need for a functioning aqueduct begged for attention: the Emberá had been planning to construct cabanas to attract tourists interested in learning about the Emberá's heritage and exploring the area's nature offerings, just as other indigenous groups have successfully accomplished in Panama.   Since Ipetí Kuna sits just across the highway, the proximity could introduce visitors to two of Panama's heritages (maybe even three, if the visitors are partial to *pollo frito*) in a three-hour drive from the capital. I was curious to see how much closer the Emberá had realized their goal, as well as seeing what role sustenance still plays in their lives. So, six months later, I returned to Ipetí with the idea of staying, if permitted, on the Emberá side.

The Peace Corps had assisted in fixing the problematic concrete and PVC aqueduct, but when I arrived, the unreliability of the exposed pipes—and the inherently feeble water source—continued. Nor were the cabanas built yet. After asking if it were possible to stay anywhere else in the village, a family volunteered to take me in for $5 per night, plus $2 per meal.

An attractively vibrant young couple, Hector and Luz Estrella ("star light" in English), led me up a notched log serving as a ladder into their pole house, smaller than a trailer home, and proving much breezier than Kuna dwellings, since it had no walls, except a small closet that had been constructed off to one side. The raised floor, with its slats 4 feet from the ground and about half an inch apart from one another, remained cool even at noontime.

The roof's underbelly wore a black stain above the fogon, the firewood pit atop the floor where Luz prepared the meals. Owing to age-old indigenous engineering, rainwater does not enter through the roof, yet the smoke from the fogon escapes easily through the leaves of the thatch while, at the same time, smoking out any squatting critters that might have taken refuge inside its folds.

Following a simple architectural motif, the floor remained open and clear since the roof beams supported a collection of household amenities. A pair of branches, suspended by rope above the fogon like trapezes, served as meat smokers. A sack of rice seeds dangled punching bag-style from the roof to keep rats away from its tasty bounty. With its lazy, breeze-guided swing, a hammock whispered "siesta."

Whimpers of Corazon, their pet parrot, emanated from around the fogon, the bird's favorite begging platform. Below, dreaming dogs sprawled themselves out in the afternoon sun like laundry blown off a clothesline. Under the planks of the raised floor, roosters proudly humped chickens, ignoring the hens' flaps and squeals of protest, all but assuring the cycle of nature will continue to provide fresh animal protein for the household.

While keeping to many traditions, the couple has also opted for a few Western conveniences, most notably, a bare light bulb swinging from the ceiling. From 6 p.m. to 10 p.m. every day, Ipetí Emberá has electricity, courtesy of the village's prize acquisition, a rasp-roaring kerosene generator, and its corresponding network of wires slung above the footpaths.

But, alas, as with other Western conveniences, the generator generates expenses as well. Aside from a few crafts the couple creates in their spare time—Luz weaving intricate baskets and Hector carving local fauna out of ivory-colored tagua nuts— Hector was earning most of the household's share of the generator bill by clearing fields with machetes to prepare them for crops. Along with a homemade dumbbell Hector built by dipping a metal bar into buckets of concrete, the nature of his labor helped maintain his muscular frame, marred only with a gash above his left bicep.   A month ago, while clearing dense brush, he accidentally sliced open his arm with a swing of the machete, sending him 10 bloody miles to the nearest equipped medical center for stitches. But when I met him, he was already lifting his concrete dumbbell again. Back to work.

*   *   *

The Emberá are no strangers to currency, although their relationship with it has forever changed.   As observed by Per Høst, a Norwegian scientist who traveled to the isthmus in the late 1940s, the Emberá of eastern Panama used to collect coins as payment, only to artfully string the glistening coins into intricate jewelry. I can't say I had seen any quarters dangling around the necks of any Emberá I had met in Panama (except for a few faux coin necklaces), although now the metal currency can certainly be heard ringing in the pockets of their shorts.

Hector, like many other men of the village, kept his wardrobe stocked with shorts instead of a lineup of colorful loincloths, the latter being the timeless fashion choice of a few Emberá seniors (and Emberá youth from some tourist-ready villages). As for the sartorial shift of the women, only a few of the elders of the village still shunned shirts. Luz preferred sleeveless tops and vibrant, machine-made prints for wrapping into skirts. A porch of one house in the village doubled as a thrift store, hawking whatever used garments came down the road from the highway.

However viewed, the importance of local fashion should not be underrated. Earlier, I had mentioned that the currency of Panama is the U.S. dollar (with Panamanian-issued coinage of equal value) yet, in rural Panama, currency effectively becomes whatever you are carrying. For sure, cash is always welcome, but in expanses with no post offices, no Internet, and no banks, your cache of cooking oil, books, and unused batteries suddenly convert you into a talking trading post. One day, I bartered away an American-made, monster truck t-shirt for a tagua nut carving at the village's fledgling crafts store, and the artist accepted without hesitation. I did my best to contribute to the area's robust circulation of merchandise, with a little help from Bigfoot the 4x4.

* * *

My first meal in Hector and Luz's care provided a glistening example of the tangle of cultures that has become Ipetí Emberá. I experienced the sweetness of fresh rice and the *al dente* texture of fresh beans—an unforgettable thrill of flavor missing from their dried supermarket counterparts—infused with smoke from the wood fire and accompanied by cubed Panamanian mystery meat from a can—and all the while watching the evening news in Spanish on the couple's jungle-side television.

I gave the couple a bottle of dark rum, with which Hector promptly returned the favor and poured us both a shot. Luz chose not to partake, for as the evening approached, the television station began its nightly lineup of Spanish soap operas. Soon, a collection of women young and old from the village climbed into the house and gathered around the television, while men, young and old, approached the table, poked unlit cigarettes into the flame of the fogon, and gathered around the bottle of rum. The elixir spun up a makeshift school using Spanish as the conduit, where the villagers taught me words in the Emberá language, while I shared words of English in return.

Meanwhile, the village's leader, Pacho, turned up with a corn-oil jug refilled with the traditional Emberá home brew, *wiki*, fermented from corn and sugar. He admitted that the jug's contents, just a small scoop from a 10-gallon batch, was a little young and needed a few more days to reach its normal potency. He then proceeded to mix the jug's bounty with a bottle of *seco* I added to the table, creating a popular drink that boasts both an Emberá name—*champoriao*—and a Spanish name—*veinte veinte*, or 20/20. As the women at the other end of the house quietly sat and reunited with the overdramatic characters of the soap opera *Gitanas*, the men explained the drink's Spanish name to me: since the young *wiki's* sweetness masks its strength, the mixture appears to bestow the drinker with 20/20 vision.

And crisp eyesight would prove beneficial. The generator snapped out of its distant chug and began thrashing, slowly crying itself to death, while the bulbs of the Emberá houses faded and flashed in sympathy with each grinding oscillation, until it gave up in a dramatic wail. The house and the jungle melted together in a dark peace. And right in the middle of *Gitanas*!

Peppering the blackness with Spanish and Emberá chatter, flashlight beams jiggling about, a reconnaissance party left the house, bound for the generator's hut. It turned out that the nomenclature of the Emberá specialty 20/20 seemed to ring true: we all agreed that guided by flashlights, we saw rather clearly, although we couldn't walk all that straight.

After a fellow had coaxed the generator back into operation, the women barely missed a mascara-laced sob of the *Gitanas* protagonists before the television's soldered innards began to faithfully pump and flicker with the jolt of the generator. But the other side of the house had met with a new impasse: the bottle of *seco* that I had brought was empty.   "Where is the bottle's grandfather?" Pacho mused, referring to the more common liter bottles of the Panamanian distillant.

Another house in the village doubles as a small grocery store (every village seems to have at least one of those), so I gave one of the young men $5 and he returned with the grandfather bottle of *seco* with which to accompany the remaining hours of electricity. "To the grandfather," we toasted, almost respectfully.

Commercials for Spanish soaps with such names as "Real Love" aired into the open-walled dwelling. With the lucidity of *veinte veinte* at the helm, laughter fell into cackles, and language fell into disuse.   The more couth half of the house fared better, however; a 5-year-old girl peering up at the television inquired, "What is real love?"

* * *

Free of the urban affliction of nighttime car alarms, I fell asleep to the dueling lullabies of rodents clawing about on the roof and a rooster sounding off right below me through the planks of the house's floor.   But another even more ubiquitous troublemaker remained absent from the evening's jungle ensemble: the mosquito, the queen of malaria and the vaccine-elusive dengue fever, albeit nowadays, carriers of such misfortune remain remote. Ipetí Emberá remains free of them, even though just a mile to the north, the whippet-fueled buzz of the bloodsuckers torments Ipetí Kuna.   Luz credited their pesk-free air to a bulwark of mosquito-repelling herbs planted by the villagers.

A breakfast of fried plantains and a tea steeped from a stalk shaped like a chive, but smelling like lemon, provided energy for the morning's task: fishing.   But if you ask the villagers, they'd tell you that they would not be out catching fish, but in refreshing candor, "killing fish."

Fishing—make that killing—was not a solitary rod-and-bobber affair. An entourage of half a dozen villagers, with a Yankee in tow, set out upstream with a 30-foot net, several spears, and a few snorkel masks, all balanced in a top-heavy dugout canoe scarcely wider than a frying pan. I was not surprised that Per Høst had likened riding in an Emberá river canoe to rope dancing.

Cane poles pushed us up over a mile against the current to position us far enough upstream to reach the cleaner water above patches of Ipetí Colono farmland and cow pasture, and above whoever was washing clothes or taking a bath next to the village. At the desired location—an elbow in the river—they strung the net from one bank to the other. While two people drew the net towards the elbow, the spear team strapped on goggles and moved in on the trapped prey. It wasn't long before one young, ribby fishkiller emerged shouting, a wide-mouthed grin pushing up his goggles, and an impaled tilapia squirming on his spear. "The power of 20/20!" he gloated.

But the spear didn't kill the fish all the time. After the first fishkiller knocked his catch off the spear and into the narrowness of the canoe—no plastic cooler to hold the catch here—the fish tried to flap its way out. It almost succeeded. Since I was still sitting in the canoe, observing the technique of the spear hunters, I figured I'd better finish the reaper's job before the bounty escaped back into the river. That was when I learned how many knife stabs a tilapia can withstand before accepting death and how sharp their needle-like fins are. Soon, the canoe was filling up with pissed off fish and a mixture of their blood and my blood, the ratio of which difficult to discern, since our heart juices appeared uncannily alike. It was a humbling moment that could have served as a reflective experience for the caste of vegetarians who won't eat animal meat but will happily scarf down fish. Where is the distinction drawn? At the number of the creature's heart chambers?

Hector asked me if I wished to try spearing. A year ago, I had met with giddy success fishing without a rod for jurel off an island in the Kuna Yala archipelago, using only a hand-manipulated fishing line and squid for bait, so why not try to spear my lunch this time? Moreover, Hector had made the task appear so fluid and satisfying. Taking a break from scaling the fish in the boat, I jumped into the water, strapped on the snorkel mask, and slipped my eyelids into my best predatory contortion. When I wasn't perturbing the riverbed into an opaque brown cloud with lumbering steps, I spied a few tilapias spying me. Every time I attempted to move within spearing distance, they were two fins ahead of me and shot off into safety, while snickering, no doubt.

Now that the tilapias were safe from my clumsiness, I began to pick on some small fry hiding near the rocks on the bottom. I didn't care whether they were a particularly tasty species or not. I would eat them anyway. The most primitive tissue of my brain stem was quivering recklessly, commanding me to rack one up.

But I only ended up dulling Hector's spear when it struck rocks instead of the fish that managed to disappear before impact. The villagers, on the other hand, had caught enough tilapia to provide lunch for everyone—a good thing, since I had only managed to spear a leaf. At the very least, I secured a bath out of the experience, since the aqueduct was dry that day.

Before we could dine, chores awaited. But who needs soap when one possesses knowledge of the diverse Central American jungle? The group scoured the nearby greenery and picked leaves off of a plant, *palo rojo,* appearing as any scrawny shrub, but when rubbed vigorously, the green pulp lathered into a refreshing, cleansing froth.

Back at the riverbank of the village, Hector dunked the canoe in the river to rid it of unsightly scales and blood. He and another knife-slapping villager stood half submerged in the river, cleaning and scoring the fish, as a 6-year-old girl, barely taller than the machete in her hand, observed and mimicked the technique of the adults; another nugget of Emberá culture passes down to a younger generation. Discarded fins and scraps, taken downstream by the current, boiled in scrums of red-nosed sardines, which attacked the floating detritus with frantic delight.

Fueled by branches Luz had macheted off during the return trip, the fogon hosted the tilapia in bubbling vegetable oil, seasoned only with salt. After inclusion of a dollop of fresh rice, the crispy tilapia required nothing else to complete the popular Emberá meal.

* * *

After a few nights in the Darién province, I was returning to the capital and stopped in Ipetí. One of Luz and Hector's chickens was upstairs, relieved of its feathers and its head. The village hummed with its latest news: a stronger source for the aqueduct had been located. Ipetí Kuna and Ipetí Emberá may have daily potable water yet.

But that wasn't the only news. Across the highway, I met a young Ipetí Kuna man who, as a city-trained guide, would be hosting Ipetí Kuna's first ever tour group from Panama City the next day. The guide, Igua, explained to me in perfect English that instead of having to fly to one of the islands of Kuna Yala, entailing at least an overnight stay, tourists toting bottled water could hop on an air-conditioned tour bus in Panama City for a three-hour drive and view Ipetí Kuna's *chicha* house, observe a traditional Kuna dance, and learn how the Kuna dry coffee beans in the sun in preparation for the market, among other introductions to the Kuna culture. The visitors could also enjoy guided nature hikes around the comarca's forest that still claims a bustling population of tropical birds. Soon, tourists will have the chance to visit a museum of Kuna culture, to be built in the village.

Since Ipetí Emberá lies across the highway, and was planning its cabanas, Igua planned cooperation on future tour groups, and was already in contact with them. Thus two historical archenemies of the isthmus will soon join forces to capitalize on a change that had uprooted both of their lives—proximity to Panamanian culture, the highway, and the city.

We spoke under the shade of the fruit stand's zinc roof near the bus stop. As he teased the slippery white pulp off the seeds of a guama pod harvested from the village's fincas, Igua explained to me why tourism would be important for the community. The income from tourism would assist the Madungandi comarca so that it would not need to sell trees inside its borders to chain saw-fortified *colonos*, a practice hastened because most of the forest near Madungandi had already been shorn clean, leading the *colonos* to offer money to the comarca for the resource. More income would also provide better patrolling of the border, since the government, according to Igua, had done nothing to stop the illegal activity of some *colonos* felling trees inside the comarca without permission.

Ironically, capital, normally viewed as a cold-hearted killer of tradition, could help preserve part of the jungle—and, hence, indigenous culture—rather than destroy it. The indigenous Ipetí communities will soon, we would hope, have a choice as to what degree they wish to further incorporate the Western way of life into their own, a choice many other indigenous communities across the Americas do not enjoy.

Igua gave me a guama pod, but did not reveal his trick for separating the stretchy pulp—sweet like vanilla ice cream—from the seeds. Many awkward lingual manipulations later, I noticed that a few women sitting behind us at the fruit stand had paused from their embroidery for a little giggly chatter. Igua joined their enjoyment and said to me, "They said that you chew it like a baby."

They would soon receive a bus full of guama-chewing entertainment.

15.

The Little Goat

THE PAN-AMERICAN HIGHWAY meanders over 25,000 kilometers from Alaska to Tierra del Fuego, except for a break—the only one—at the mountainous jungle between Panama and Colombia. On the Panamanian side, the party town of Yaviza celebrates its distinction at the end of the road with its troupes of salsa-stepping storeowners and humping stray dogs strewn about its walkways. For more communal recreational pursuits, the town's open-aired cockfighting palace holds seating for 80. Yaviza is the rowdy border town without the border.

Kids running around the ruins of a Spanish fort-turned-playground greeted me, ignoring the police choppers that thumped above. Without roads, the police and their AK-47s require the helicopters, along with small, agile boats, to travel further east into the lawless bonanza known as the Darién Gap, where an assortment of Colombian guerrilla factions have trickled in and hunkered down. Despite over half a century's talk of extending the highway all the way to the boundary with Colombia (30 miles away), recent Panamanian concerns about the accelerated influx of drugs, Colombian civil war elements, and hoof-and-mouth disease, not to mention the inevitable ecological damage, have thus far kept the Darién Gap an unforgiving jungle.

As willing boatmen abounded, I was able to reach a few nearby indigenous Emberá villages in the comarca north of the town to examine their recovery from a recent flood — my main objective. But without the requisite AK-47, I wasn't prepared to venture eastward into the Gap. And since I had reached my fill of dancehall beats bounding out of the open concrete walls of Yaviza's bars until 3 a.m. and starting up again at sunrise (as was the case with the venue right below my fan-cooled, hostel-style room), I was left with no particular eagerness to remain in town. Did that make me a party pooper? Was I supposed to warm up to the crudely painted pictures of women in their underwear on the walls of the bars?

Yaviza thought so. I must have offended her, for as I was to discover, she would make it difficult to leave.

Planning my escape, I first looked to Panama's fleet of *diablos rojos*, the ex-American school buses painted as gaudily as the drivers' personalities dictate. Shrouded in airbrushed cartoon characters and names of girlfriends, the buses provide public transport to and from some of the most far-reaching villages across the isthmus, including Yaviza, nine hours from the capital, down a road still lacking pavement for the last four hours of the trip. Then again, three-fourths of Panama's people do not own automobiles, lavishing great importance on the country's buses that dutifully prowl a road system remaining two-thirds unpaved. I have logged many an exhaust-festooned hour inside *diablos rojos* and other permutations of Panamanian public buses while speakers mounted in the ceiling kept the passengers groovin' to salsa, Panamanian *típico*, or even American classic rock. Legroom deficiencies aside, I was actually looking forward to the ride.

But by the early afternoon, the bus drivers' workday was done. After nine hours, the diesel engines of *diablos rojos* that had already arrived from the capital earned a break, their combustive gnarling silenced for the rest of the day. Their vivid paint jobs would fade in the sun of Yaviza until the next morning. The capital-bound buses, likewise, had all left hours ago, before the sun had risen. The afternoon was time for the bus drivers to enjoy a few cold beers and place some earnings on one of Yaviza's badass cocks. So how, at that balmy hour, could I return to the capital without a car?

An hour's canoe ride south could have taken me to a rustic airstrip, but a crash of a local commercial flight a month ago elsewhere in the country and the subsequent shortage of planes had shoved schedules down an abyss of futility. I decided to pass on the frequent flier miles.

I still had one option. But it would only carry me part of the way back. Enterprising farmers, keeping with the idea of recycling ancient automobiles that should have been melted down into scrap, have been converting trucks into buses by constructing passenger cabins on the backs of the trucks' flatbeds. Panamanians refer to the franken-vehicles as *chivas*, or little goats—an appropriate label considering the type of unsavory, all-dirt terrain they were designed to ply.

As the afternoon blazed unhindered, Yavizans sucked the sweat off their lips and promised me in between unrushed grins that a *chiva* would turn up soon. Over the next couple hours, several burly trucks arrived, circled around, and left. All were transports shuffling heavily armed Panamanian policemen to and from their base in town. But where was the bus for unarmed civilians?

"There's the *chiva*," a vendor gestured to me from his reclined paunch, sinking behind his table of batteries and plastic toys. He was pointing to an approaching truck, a pickup truck.

Five bucks would get me two and a half hours back up the highway to Meteti, the driver of the 4x4 told me, as I climbed in to the truck bed adorned with a tarpaulin atop two wooden benches that he didn't bother to fasten down. There were no speakers, hence no *típico*. Joining a half dozen passengers hanging onto the tarpaulin posts, I straddled a spare wheel and a scattering of wanton corn kernels from a past rider, just before the Yaviza-Metetí local turned around and jostled back onto the Pan-American Highway, in all its single lane, unpaved glory.

Yaziva is so far away from the rest of the country that the loggers and farmers who have shorn most of the land surrounding the highway clean of anything round and tall haven't completed clearing all the jungle near the terminal town. But the loggers are getting close. Just a few wiggles of the bench later, we eased past open cattle ranches. Even the jungle of the distant mountains, miles away from the roadway, had been converted to pasture. Some of the slopes rose so sharply, I wondered if the grazing cows had to wear crampons just so someone could enjoy a filet mignon, just about the only cut of a Panamanian-raised cow not normally requiring a meat grinder to attain edibility. At least the animals were getting their exercise. In the end, however, the destruction of the habitats of hundreds of tropical birds, reptiles, animals, insects, and plants has only resulted in producing chewy steak — perhaps nature is laughing last after all.

Neither the bouncing of the rear axle nor the roving bench prevented a mother across from me from opening a bottle of Squirt soda, filling a baby bottle with it, and promptly serving it to the infant straddling her thigh. The baby, wearing nothing but a diaper and a bumpy rash on his neck, slurped down the soda without losing a drop to the vehicle's convulsions. Lucky mother — the *chiva* must have burped the baby for her.

Since the tarpaulin only covered the top and sides of the cabin, the open front and back allowed in anything the highway decided to send our way. When a vehicle passed, shooting a jet of fresh dust under the tarpaulin, everyone in the *chiva* instinctively tucked in helpless grimaces. Like the spreading of an unchecked disease, the dust of the dirtway painted everything within 20 feet of it with its pale auburn likeness—fence posts, leaves of palm trees, grazing cows, everything.

The dryness of the road proved pestering, but I was fortunate the rainy season had not yet begun. If it had, the daily afternoon drenchings, according to Yavizans, turn this part of the highway into a sludge monster, passable to only the most talented *chiva* driver. The much heavier and less nimble *diablos rojos* often become stuck up to their axles in the mud.

A straw-hatted passenger rapped on the roof of the cab—the *chiva* equivalent of "it's my stop." Each side of the roof donned a shallow, fist-sized indentation, the hallmark of a well-used *chiva*. At the same stop, a few saddle-faced farmers climbed aboard with their machetes, and another hoisted a tank of kerosene into the pickup bed. Knees bent with innovative topology to accommodate. The coveted passenger seat inside the pickup cab, reserved apparently for either mobility-restricted grandmothers or comely young ladies, acquired a passenger fitting an appropriate criterion of the latter variety. We lost a little off our pace until she was delivered a mile down the road.

But she mattered not compared to our regular yielding for crossing caravans of dogs, oblivious chickens, goats, and frogs the size of softballs. Freshly cut spoils of loggers lay along the side of the road, sometimes spilling onto it, providing additional fodder for brake pads amid the concrete churches and saddle repair shops on a stretch of farmland that, just 25 years prior, was a canopied jungle.

The mother was sitting near the pickup's back door. Atop her lap, a pudgy leg of her infant flopped over the open edge. As the mother gripped the infant with one hand and the bottle of Squirt in the other, the baby appeared to be one savage bump away from becoming the load that fell of the truck.

When the frogs gave us the right of way, the driver demonstrated his prowess for clinging to the dirt at ample velocity (a grandmother was sitting in the front passenger seat, nonetheless). A mob of rocks perturbed by the pickup's tires attacked the vehicle's underbelly with a chorus of pings, lushly fitful, a hailstorm from the ground up. Inter-passenger chatter relied on quick bursts of yelling, usually something like "are you all right?" followed by levity-reassuring laughter. The remains of the suspension system sent the passengers—12 of us now—up against the support beams of the tarpaulin, as the beams flaunted talent for finding the tender meat between one's spinal discs.

Meanwhile, the baby, a wiggling jelly puppet, had employed its own defense system against the inclement environment: a nap. It was enough to make a grown man envious. Just how can babies do that? After a fellow passenger knocked on the roof for the mother, she safely climbed out of the pickup, losing neither the baby nor the bottle of Squirt from her clench worthy of a rugby player.

The path swelled wide enough for two lanes, save the occasional stretch where a landslide had dispensed with half the road. A stop sign, impaling the middle of the highway itself, failed to delay our *chiva*, the driver actually speeding up at the sign of red. The pebble ensemble responded by improvising a crescendo, as the piercing smell of slash-and-burn farming—the official scent of the Panamanian countryside—swam through the *chiva*.

With a few newly acquired, 50-pound bags of rice as ballast, the driver finished delivering his passengers and cargo, dusty but intact, to the cowboy town of Meteti, his last stop. We only traveled 30 miles, but the *chiva*—part bus, part grain silo, part baby-burper—had bucked me two and a half hours closer to the capital.

From the earthen lot doubling as the drop-off point, an unmarked pickup passed me and bounced back towards Yaviza. A few farmers stood vigilantly in the back. Their 4x4 being just a regular, private truck, it sported neither a tarpaulin nor benches. Second-class travel, I tell you.

16.
Los Santos: Where the Bulls Crash the Party

PANAMA HAS LONG BEEN KNOWN as a home of talented ballplayers — but let's not forget the *bull*players.

In the Panamanian province of Los Santos, the job market is anemic, the soil is poor and difficult for cash crops, and the roads are more pocked than an asteroid. But the people of the province still always manage to find a reason to party, especially when partying hard means fighting the bulls.

At the end of August, the community of Llano de Piedra holds their annual Santa Rosa de Lima Festival in their downtown consisting entirely of two rustic, t-shaped intersections, sans traffic lights. When I arrived by public van on the last day of the festival, the tiny ranching community was celebrating from one intersection to the other with two improvised bullrings, in between which they scattered stalls of fried fare, dusty gambling tables, and a live cumbia band competing with stereo system speakers occupying a pickup truck's entire payload. Defying — albeit fleetingly — the 33 degree C afternoon, the open-air bar stocked crates of 50-cent beers, just within the budget of the campesino's average wage of $7 per day.

Before you spin up images of tight-fitting matador costumes and poodle-ear hats, let me say that participants in a Panamanian bullfight hop into the ring with whatever they were wearing on the farm that morning. In most cases, the ring is not even a ring — it's a square pen constructed out of five-rail, cattle-corral panels, reinforced with tree posts sunk into the ground several feet. Fans of blood sports might want to stick to cockfights, because under the tropical palm trees of Panama, the object of the bullfight is not to kill the bull; the bulls are only teased with a couple ratty quilts and then get to go home. The object, so it seems, is to avoid being killed. Good exercise for both man and bull.

Even though the bulls stomp into the close-quarters pen with 900 pounds of drooling angst, the *matadors* — er, make that *jugadores* ("players") — don't rely on any arrows to weaken the bulls before the game begins, as is done in Spain, to balance the playing field. You see, the bulls in Panamanian bullfights aren't bred for fighting. They're bred for, well, breeding. The bullplayers only equalize the game by fortifying themselves with generous, dribbly swigs of 70-proof *Seco Herrerano*.

"I've been fighting the bulls for 12 years," declared Juan, an open-shirted bullplayer, in between skirmishes. He told me that he traveled from neighboring Costa Rica to party with the bulls at the Santa Rosa Festival, as we conversed through the fence gaps just small enough to prevent a bull from ramming his head into the torso of one of the many onlookers.

And speaking of onlookers, the bravado was far from reserved for the bullplayers, since many of the beer-gripping locals sat balanced on the fence's top rung, kicking the bulls in the head when the beastly breeders wandered their way. Carlos, a veteran bull*kicker*, turned his grinning face down to me and remarked, "The bulls can't jump up and hurt us way up here. We're safe." He slapped his hand on the steel railing next to him, offering me a choice spot. "Are you afraid?"

After I answered him affirmatively, I remained at ground level with the families, the curious dogs, and the skewer vendors, who dragged their hibachis next to the fencing (location, location). That was when I noticed I was the only man in shorts. Even most of the boys wore jeans, despite the town's year-round, balmy climate at a latitude of not even 8 degrees north of the equator. I was also the only one who jumped when fireworks exploded just a few feet away, behind the bull truck. Meanwhile, the party didn't miss a step. A salesman carefully weaved through the crowd, proving worthiness of his arsenal of waterproof watches by toting them around in jars filled with water. A sweet crack of billiard balls discharged from the open-aired, dust-swirled table near the bar, and then a grunt escaped from the end of the bull ramp. Next contestant, please.

As a barkeep cranked the handle of an ice crusher, the equatorial sun baked the ground, which was dusty even though it had rained heavily two days before. The grass on which the bulls romped and the bullplayers quaffed resembled that of the province's nubby, crew-cut mountains that had proudly been shaved and converted to pasture for cattle. Some mountains in the province are so steep that cows sometimes lose their footing and roll to their deaths (adding a whole new sinister dimension to cow-tipping, I suppose). The name Llano de Piedra—literally Stone Plain—speaks honestly about the town's unusually flatter geography, as well as the difficulty the campesinos have had in growing crops.

Stripped of the natural variety and bounty of tropical plant matter—both live and decaying—the pasture's soil, as scientist Benjamin Turner of Panama's Smithsonian Tropical Research Institute once explained to me, becomes easily destabilized and dries quickly. From the point of view of a bullplayer, however, this might not be a bad thing. "Mud, that's no good for bullfighting anyway," a spectator pointed out under his straw *pintado* hat as he motioned with his beer bottle. "It's dangerous if the bullfighter slips."

As Juan taunted his next hoofed counterpart around the pen alongside Chino, an equally dexterous, jeans-clad bullplayer from the province, a third bullplayer lassoed the bull's horns in a perfect rope toss, sending the animal back up the exit ramp. Recess was over for the bull, but another groaning bovine soon sloppily dove into the pen with a boy hanging onto his back, riding him like a pony. No saddle, no reigns—just an adventurous sense of fun.

The next bull, searching zealously for the party to which he had been listening from the inside of a cattle truck, slammed his boulder of a head into one of the pen's corners, slightly but ominously jarring loose a few posts. The true fans knew a substandard support when they saw it; no one had been sitting atop that corner all day.

At the end of the afternoon's bull procession, the only casualties were a few livers, and perhaps a couple dice-chucking gamblers who lost more money than the ground lost topsoil. The people of the town gave their patron saint a good show.

While most Los Santos hotels remain packed during the big events, like Carnival and Easter, the province's hotels reported a 7 percent occupancy rate for the entirety of 2002, according to IPAT, the Tourist Institute of Panama. Not all fiestas bring in the bulls, but since the agrarian province holds hundreds of fiestas every year (760, according to one historian), you should be able to find a party where a *santeño* is saving you a choice seat atop the railing.

Bibliography

Aceto, Michael. "Variation in a Secret Creole Language in Panama." *Language and Society* 24: 537-560, 1995.

----. "A New Creole Future Tense Marker Emerges on the Panamanian West Indies." *American Speech* 73:1 29-43, 1998.

"Administration support for 1989 US Invasion Victims." *Central America Report,* 20 January 1995.

Angulo, Yamileth and Lomonte, Bruno. "Inhibitory effect of fucoidan on the activities of crotaline snake venom myotoxic phospholipases A2." *Biochemical Pharmacology* 66:10 p1993-2000, 2003.

Berrocal, R.E. "Prohíben comercio de animales con Panamá." *La Prensa,* 18 May 2004 (http://mensual.prensa.com/mensual/contenido/2004/05/18/hoy/portada/1689408.html).

Campbell, Jonathan A. and Lamar, William W. *The Venomous Reptiles of the Western Hemisphere.* Volume 1. Ithaca: Comstock Publishing Associates, 2004.

Castillero, Ernesto J. *The Legends and Stories of Old Panama.* Panama: Producciones Erlizca, 1999. Translated by Eloy A Fisher H.

Castillo, Arcadio; and Lessios, H.A. "Lobster Fishery by the Kuna Indians in the San Blas Region of Panama (Kuna Yala). *Crustaceana* 74:5 459-475, 2001.

Clagett, Brian. "Life History of the Sea Turtle." *The Newsletter of the Colorado Herpetological Society* 29:5, 2002 (http://coloherp.org/cb-news/Vol-29/cbn-0205/SeaTurtle.php).

Cobb, C.E. "Panama: Ever at the crossroads." *National Geographic* 169:4 467–493, 1986.

Columbus, Christopher. *Four Voyages to the New World.* London: Citadel Press, 1961.

Columbus, Ferdinand. *The Life of the Admiral Christopher Columbus by his Son Ferdinand.* Translated by Benjamin Keen. London: the Folio Society, 1960.

Convention on International Trade in Endangered Species. "Djibouti, Equatorial Guinea, Guinea-Bissau, Liberia, Mozambique, Panama, Rwanda and Sierra Leone — Recommendation to suspend trade." CITES Notification # 2004 / 024 of 30 April 2004. (http://www.cites.org/eng/notifs/2004/024.pdf).

Cowley, Goeffrey and Talbot, Mary. "The Great Disease Migration." *Newsweek* 118:10 p54, 1991.

Daly, John W and Myers, Charles W. "Toxicity of Panamanian Poison Frogs (Dendrobates): Some Biological and Chemical Aspects." *Science*, New Series, 156 (No. 3777) 970-973, 1967.

Dinges, John. *Our Man in Panama*. New York: Random House, 1990.

Doggett, Scott. *Panama*. London: Lonely Planet Publications, 2001.

Downer, S. 1996. "Iguana: Survival of the tastiest." *Iguana Times* 5: 16–18 (reprinted from Costa Rica Today, 21 October 1993).

Eilers, K., W. Koops, H. Udo, H. Van Keulen, and J. Noordhuizen. Analysis of Iguana iguana farming systems in Nicaragua, Costa Rica, and Panama. *Interciencia* 27: 599–606, 2002.

"El Parque Nacional Marino de Isla Bastimentos." *La Prensa* 18 May 2003 (http://mensual.prensa.com/mensual/contenido/2003/05/18/hoy/nacional es/962898.html).

"Existencia de Animales en la República, por Clase de Animal: 22 de Abril de 2001." Panama: Direccion de Estadística y Censo, 2001.

"FAOSTAT data, 2005." Food and Agriculture Organization of the United Nations, 2005 (http://faostat.fao.org).

Graham, Gladys R. *Tropical Cooking: A Handbook of Tropical Foods and How to Use Them*. Panama City: The Panama American Press, 1947.

Greene, Graham. *Getting to Know the General: The Story of an Involvement*. Thorndike, Maine: Thorndike Press, 1984.

Goode, Richard U. "A Trip to Panama and Darien." *National Geographic* 1:4 301-314, 1889.

Gunner Schull, Helen; Kingsland Woodruff, Marjorie; and Caramano de Sucre, Yolanda (editors). *Living at the Crossroads: a guide to the Isthmus of Panama*. Panama: Imprenta Nacional, 1957.

Guzman, Hector M.; Guevara, Carlos; and Castillo, Arcadio. "Natural Disturbances and Mining of Panamanian Coral Reefs by Indigenous People." *Conservation Biology* 17:5 1396-1401, 2003.

Haskin, Frederic J. *The Panama Canal*. New York: Doubleday, Page & Company, 1913.

Howe, James. *A People Who Would Not Kneel: Panama, the United States, and the San Blas Kuna*. Washington D.C.: Smithsonian Institution Press, 1998.

Høst, Per. *Children of the Jungle*. London: Pan Books Ltd., 1956.

Jackson, Eric. *9°N: Dispatches from Panama, 1994-2000*. Panama City: Panama News Books, 2000.

----. "ACOBIR wants closer scrutiny of Bocas, Boquete real estate." *The Panama News* 10:24, 2004

(http://www.thepanamanews.com/pn/v_10/issue_24/business_briefs.html)
.

----. "Mireya and her gang on the run." *The Panama News* 10:21, 2004 (http://www.thepanamanews.com/pn/v_10/issue_21/news_03.html).

----. "Saving traditional knowledge." *The Panama News* 9:20, 2003 (http://www.thepanamanews.com/pn/v_09/issue_20/science_01.html).

Labrut, Michèle. *Getting to Know Panama*. Panama City: Focus Publications, 1997.

Kempe, Frederick. *Divorcing the Dictator: America's Bungled Affair with Noriega*. New York: G.P. Putnam's Sons, 1990.

Manegold, C.S. "A Standoff in Panama: Noriega takes sanctuary in Vatican Embassy, and the United States brings pressure on Rome." *Newsweek* 115:2 p 28, 1990.

McCullough, David. *The Path between the Seas*. New York: Simon & Schuster, 1977.

Miller, Tom. *The Panama Hat Trail*. Washington, D.C.: National Geographic Adventure Press, 2001.

National Marine Fisheries Service and U.S. Fish and Wildlife Service. "Recovery Plan for U.S. Pacific Populations of the Olive Ridley Turtle (Lepidochelys olivacea)." National Marine Fisheries Service, Silver Spring, MD, 1998.

National Research Council. "Agouti," pp. 199-206; and "Green Iguana," pp. 347-353. In: *Microlivestock: Little-Known Small Animals with a Promising Economic Future*. National Academy Press, Washington, D.C, 1991.

Noriega, Manuel and Eisner, Peter. *America's Prisoner: The Memoirs of Manuel Noriega*. New York: Random House, 1997.

Noto, José. *Historia de El Valle Antón, Segunda Edición*. Colombia: 2001.

Oakes, Perry J. *A Description of Teribe Phonology*. SIL International, 2001.

"Panama: Country Reports on Human Rights Practices - 2002." The Bureau of Democracy, Human Rights, and Labor, March 31, 2003. (http://www.state.gov/g/drl/rls/hrrpt/2002/18340.htm).

"Por la Cual se Crea la Comarca Naso Tjer Di." Proyecto 019, Anteproyecto 021, Asamblea Legislative Secretaría General, September, 2004 (http://www.asamblea.gob.pa/buscador/proyectos/2004_P_019.pdf).

"Principales Indicadores Sociodemográficos y Económicos de la Población de la República, Por Provincia, Distrito, Corregimiento y Lugar Poblado: Censo 2000." Panama: Direccion de Estadística y Censo, 2001 (http://www.contraloria.gob.pa/dec/Aplicaciones/POBLACION_VIVIEND A/lug_poblados02/frame.htm).

Rand, A.S., B.A. Dugan, H. Monteza, and D. Vianda. "The diet of a generalized folivore: Iguana iguana in Panama." *Journal of Herpetology* 24 211-214, 1990.

Sánchez, Diómedes and Grinard, Migdalia. "Confabulación de las imprudencias: sangre y muerte en la carretera hacia Colón." *La Prensa*, 9 September, 2005 (http://mensual.prensa.com/mensual/contenido/2005/09/29/hoy/nacional es/353566.html).

Sara, Solomon I. *A tri-lingual dictionary of Embera-Spanish-English.* München: Lincom Europa, 2001.

Showalter, William J. "The Panama Canal." *National Geographic* 23:2 195-205, 1912.

Sklar, Holly. *Washington's War on Nicaragua.* Boston: South End Press, 1988.

Snow, Peter. "The Case for Diglossia on the Panamanian Island of Bastimentos." *Journal of Pidgin and Creole Languages* 15:1 165-169, 2000.

"This Land is My Land." *Central America Report,* 6 October 1995, p. 6.

Wali, Alaka. "In Eastern Panama, Land is the Key to Survival." *Cultural Survival Quarterly* 13:3, 1989.

Welton, Nathan. "Bites of Passage." *Natural History* 111:8 80, 2002.

Ventocilla, Jorge; Herrera, Heraclio; and Núñez, Valerio. *Plants and Animals in the Life of the Kuna.* Translated by Elisabeth King. Austin: University of Texas Press, 1995.

Index

After graduating from Columbia University, Darrin DuFord began working as a software developer when he co-founded the New York City band Motor Betty, performing on the Jenny Jones Show and across venues on both American coasts. He has since channeled his wanderlust into travel articles for such publications as *Transitions Abroad* and *Iguana*. He lives in Queens, New York. Contact him at **darrin_duford (at) hotmail.com**.

Printed in the United States
78070LV00003B/132